# JOBMANSHIP

# S. R. Redford

Macmillan Publishing Co., Inc.

NEW YORK

# JOBMANSHIP

How to Get Ahead

by "Psyching Out" Your

Boss and Co-Workers

Macmillan Publishing Co., Inc.
866 Third Avenue, New York, N.Y. 10022
Collier Macmillan Canada, Ltd.

Library of Congress Cataloging in Publication Data
Fader, Shirley Sloan.
Jobmanship.
Includes bibliographical references.
1. Success. 2. Organizational behavior. I. Title.
HF5386.F22    1978        650'.1        78–12035
ISBN 0–02–601410–6

First Printing 1978

Designed by Jack Meserole

Printed in the United States of America

In loving memory of my father,

SAMUEL LOUIS SLOAN, M.D., F.A.C.S.*—

healer of the sick; a kind, good man

*Fellow of the American College of Surgeons

# CONTENTS

# INTRODUCTION

## How Is This Jobmanship Book Different from Other Job-Success Books?

The advice in this book is different from the advice in other job-success books because every bit of it is practical and "takeable." When in 1971 *Family Weekly* commissioned the "Jobmanship" column on which this book is based, they insisted that their millions of readers wanted "practical job-success advice that people could go right out and use."

Therefore, in this book you will find no glittering business-book generalities, no success-formula jargon, no excess padding to encumber good, useable ideas, and no ivory-tower view of human relations.

What you will find are real problems, worries, and anxieties of on-the-job human relations discussed and probed for their hidden psychological meanings; then clearly, concisely answered.

## Is This Book for You?

If you sigh with boredom over job how-to books with chapter after chapter of loosely organized discussion that makes you struggle to locate the "point," then this book is for you.

If you're a man or woman who:

1. Has co-workers;
2. Is a boss or supervisor;

this book is for you.

You can be an office worker, executive, salesperson, supervisor, employed professional, technician. *No matter what your job level —from first rung to high executive*—unless you're a chairperson of the board, you have a supervisor or "boss" above you whom you must satisfy. Again, no matter what your job, you have co-workers or peers at or near your job level whom you must get along with in order to do your day's work successfully.

This book tells you how to understand, improve, and "psyche out" your on-the-job relationships with your supervisors and co-workers so you can succeed and move ahead.

## Where Did the Advice and Information in This Book Come From?

The advice and information in this book is based on interviews with industrial psychologists and leading management experts, together with the gleanings of a six-year survey of some of the best ideas published in major management and psychological books and journals. This brings us to another difference between this book and other job-success books. The other books almost always represent the ideas and theories of only one person, the author. This book represents the distilled wisdom of many experts.

Who is the author? The S. R. Redford by-line symbolizes the efforts of two people. The principal author is a widely published writer and career/job expert who specializes in the psychology of job behavior and of social behavior, both research and applied psychology. In addition to writing, she has been a business consultant, a career seminar leader, and guest lecturer at colleges.

The other half of the S. R. Redford team reviewed each chapter and contributed insights and facts. He is a Wharton M.B.A. with over twenty-five years' experience as a management consultant and executive in office and factory. Starting as a department supervisor, he moved up to become an executive vice-president and has headed several corporate divisions. Recipient of an AMA award for his "contribution to the philosophy of education for management," he chairs and lectures at many American Management Associations' seminars, serves as an American Arbitration Association panelist, and is an associate professor of management.

## How Useful Can This Book Be to You?

Read through the table of contents and recognize many on-the-job problems which you yourself have struggled with. Then turn to the appropriate pages to find in clear, straightforward form some realistic, useable solutions. *Jobmanship: How to Get Ahead by "Psyching Out" Your Boss and Co-Workers* is a book to read through for pleasure and information now. It is a book to own as a permanent guidebook to return to again and again as you encounter new job problems in your daily work life.

# JOBMANSHIP

# Problem Co-Workers: How to Cope and Win 1

It's sad. But lots of people still mistakenly believe their careers, their promotions, and their success depend on how well they do their jobs!

These people work conscientiously but somehow they never seem to be offered the promotion, the better assignment, or even a salary that matches their efforts. While they watch in anguish, the office politicians, the yes-men, and the other favorites surge ahead.

The year 1890 is officially accepted by historians as representing the close of the American Western frontier. Just as our land frontier came to an end, so the era of the rugged individualist in business has petered out. With rare exceptions, most of us now go to work in a job scene dominated by the "organization man," the "gamesman," and Riesman's other-directed "lonely crowd." In short, most of us are no longer individualistic entrepreneurs. We're part of a "team." Even people who work on individual tasks require the cooperation and goodwill of others in the company in order to do their jobs well.

Today men and women, *at any job level*, who cannot easily get along with co-workers find themselves banished to the role of outsider. Not only are they locked out and talked about, but by being isolated from the office grapevine they never hear the valuable tidbits that would have alerted them to job pitfalls or promotion opportunities. Even if it never reaches open warfare, when there's friction between co-workers—let's say between you and a co-worker—you suffer.

The report you need, the memo, the phone message, are often "forgotten" or delivered hours late. The favor that would help you through a crisis is withheld. The fragment of business information that would turn your current project into a success is never passed on. Maybe it's not even as clear-cut as that. Maybe it's only a state of mild chronic friction between you and a few others. Then it becomes a subtle war of nerves in which your antagonists contrive to drag their heels or otherwise make every daily contact difficult.

One experienced job counsellor has summed it up. "In today's job world," he says, "acceptance is more important than competence. More people lose their jobs because of personality clashes than because of incompetence. Every enemy you make, even if he's a pygmy with a toothpick, will hinder you. Every ally, no matter how insignificant, will smooth your way and help you."

Office politicians, if they are incompetent, will be found out. But office politicians (i.e., people who have learned to get along with others) who are competent will rise and succeed. In addition, because they are well accepted, their work days will be pleasant for them.

Every job has its difficult co-workers. If you battle with them and insist on treating them "as they deserve," your own life will be a series of exhausting skirmishes which, ironically, will make *you* look like a crank. If you learn instead to disarm the irritating co-workers and win their cooperation, you do yourself an enormous favor. You ease your daily work life. You transform the troublesome ones from enemies to allies. Because of your new network of allies, your phone messages, memos, etc., are remembered instead of "forgotten." Whatever relevant information your co-workers have passes regularly to your in-basket and ears. When you need reasonable help, you get it.

What you have really done by learning to get along with them is transform yourself from one lone person toiling for your personal success into a job team member—all the team is now helping you and cooperating with you to ensure your success. Of course, the others don't think of themselves as laboring on your behalf. But they are.

This chapter of *Jobmanship* looks at some of the commonest types of difficult co-workers, examines their motives, and offers easy, practical things you can do to *cope and win*.

## How to Deal with Phonies and Shirkers

One of the most exasperating co-workers is the person who manages to win credit for work he or she didn't do. Your natural reaction may be to have it out with him or to march in and set the boss straight. Since neither way is likely to lead to the results you want, you'll have to use subtler methods. Dr. John Butler, a leading industrial psychologist, suggests you and any others involved send the boss a brief note about the job the phony hero has claimed for his own. In the note, just outline the contributions of each member of your work group. Give the simple facts, not accusations. After the note, you can have a straightforward discussion with the boss to straighten out the record without tearing down any individuals—including the phony hero. The point of your conversation is simply to give the credit where it's deserved. If the problem is the reverse, where one member of your work team doesn't carry his load, Dr. Butler says it's often useful to try to understand why your co-worker is failing to do his share. Does he know what is expected of him? Maybe that's the problem. Does he have an assignment he is capable of handling? A well-respected co-worker could discuss the problem with the low-producer and ask him what he feels he can do about carrying his share. Setting up the low-producer with a "buddy" who would work closely with him and teach him how to reach the desired level of production can also be useful.

### How to Handle the Gabby Co-Worker

Though social conversation on the job is one of the fringe benefits people expect and enjoy, a few co-workers talk too much. If you find someone is wasting too much of your time and making it needlessly difficult for you to keep up with your responsibilities, try these approaches:

1. When the talkative co-worker arrives, stand up from your work to greet him. Then remain standing. If you're pleasant, he can't be insulted. Yet with the two of you on your feet, it's easier to break the conversation off and move him on.
2. Copy your boss' technique for easing long-winded visitors along. Bosses often have a secretary break in to "remind" them of a "meeting" or other appointment. You can use that approach by alerting a friendly co-worker to rescue you when he/she sees you trapped by the time-waster. Your friend can remind you of "work the boss wants right away" or some other suitable statement.

3. If there's no one who can help you, start the conversation with a good-natured greeting but mention at the beginning, "Sorry, I really can't talk long. I have a lot of work." If the gabby one doesn't take the hint, it will be appropriate, after a few minutes, for you to say, "I really have to get back now." Then do so.

Of course, if sizeable portions of your time vanish each day, consider the possibility that it's your own inclination to small-talk that may be the problem.

## How to Turn Off the Person Who Is Always "Collecting"

There's one in every work force: the person who is always "collecting." Instead of feeling grateful that someone is seeing that co-workers' illnesses, bereavements, family births, weddings, etc., are acknowledged, people often resent the collector's efforts and may even turn against contributions in general. Getting the group together and deciding on a definite policy for *who, when,* and *how* you all want to give can be the solution.

*Who* and *when:* exactly which occasions will the group acknowledge—illness of co-workers only? of co-workers plus their immediate family? weddings of co-workers? of co-workers plus their immediate family? It doesn't matter how your group decides; it's having a policy that's important.

*How*—with a card? with a gift?

Anyone who has ever had an important event in his life and has received no token from the gang at work knows that being ignored does hurt. As a result, most people are willing to give if only it doesn't seem endless and formless. Once you decide on a policy, the "collector" in your group can be put in charge. Now with guidelines set by everyone, people will feel cooperative rather than put-upon when they next hear the familiar words, "I'm collecting for . . ."

## Getting Along with the Know-It-All and the VIP

Do the co-workers you're struggling with act as if they think they're VIPs? Or do they seem to believe they're workhorses who carry a heavier work load than anyone else? Or know-it-alls who know everything there is to know about the job? Once you realize who *they think* they are, you'll be able to work with them. For example, when you realize that someone sees himself as a know-it-all, you understand you're bound to fail if you try saying, "I think you might want to know . . ." Know-it-alls can't bear to admit there's anything about the job that is new to them—something they're not already aware of. They're going to be furious with a co-worker who insults their "know-everything" self-image in this way. When, instead, you make your necessary suggestion by saying that, because you know they're aware of every detail, this is something they'll want to use, you'll do better. By saying out loud that you realize they're very aware of everything about their work, you've praised and recognized the characteristics within themselves that they most value. Now they're feeling pleasant and ready to listen.

Often your natural reaction to people playing a role is an urge to "cut them down to size." It may be fun to deflate the VIP dignity, show up the know-it-all, and prove to the workhorse that he's doing no more than others; but it is often a boomerang. It only makes your on-the-job relationships difficult. Why complicate your own life (and hurt others) when understanding other people's pictures of themselves, their ambitions, and their worries can give you cooperative co-worker friends.

## Handling a Co-Worker's Incompetence Without Nagging

People working alongside you can often make or break *your* job. No matter how efficient a worker, teacher, or salesperson you are, if there's friction between you and co-workers, your supervisor may consider *you* a liability.

When a fellow worker's actions are complicating your job life, the safest approach is to avoid any hint of faultfinding. Instead, achieve what you want by letting him help you. For example: "John, I have a problem keeping up with my paperwork. Maybe you can help me. Could I have the parts-order sheets every day before lunch? I think then I could take care of them by five o'clock." This implies that you have something at stake. It's not criticism, but rather a constructive request for aid. Spoken in private to your fellow worker, it should produce results while keeping your job friendship intact.

### Coping with the Constant Complainer

It may be hard to believe, but sometimes the constant on-the-job complainers don't even realize what they're doing. Their gripes start when they want to let others know how difficult their daily job is or they use complaints to explain away their mistakes. Gradually, complaining becomes a habit.

If you'd like some relief from the steady flow of sour remarks, you can try various approaches. Whenever the complainer begins, remember urgent work you have, apologize for not having time to listen, and tune out. The complainer will soon go looking for a better audience.

Or you can answer every complaint by pointing out the "other side" of the matter. Since complainers want sympathy, not logic, they'll take their troubles elsewhere. Be careful, though, not to overuse the logical approach to the point where you make an active enemy of the complainer.

When a normally cheerful person becomes a complainer, you'll probably want to be sympathetic. Perhaps the worries are legitimate or a reflection of some important personal problem.

For the chronic complainers who make your work life difficult by replying to your reasonable job requests with an excuse or a complaint, you may want to bring out the truth. You might say, "You're such a good worker. If you're so unhappy in this job, why do you stay? You could probably get something better elsewhere." Putting it that way can jolt the complainers into better awareness of what they've been doing and may prompt a sunnier attitude.

## People Who Can't Make Up
## Their Minds

Does your work require you to deal with people in your company who can never make up their minds? Maybe it's someone on whom you have to depend for some regular job help or job information. If so, the skirmishes may be wearing you down as you attempt to develop a system for obtaining the material you need. Perhaps your problem is that you're dealing with an "avoider." In his book, *The Achievers*, Gerald D. Bell, Professor of Organizational Behavior, University of North Carolina, mentions that though avoiders can be hard workers and very nice people, your contacts with them can be exasperating unless you understand how to react.

If your problem co-worker is an avoider, first understand that his or her biggest fear is the possibility of failure. His/her major goal is staying out of trouble. Because they have so little confidence, avoiders depend on others to lead. You may feel you're being friendly and diplomatic by discussing various job ideas or methods with them or by asking them for job suggestions. But that's where your problems may begin. People with this fear of failure will do anything to *avoid* making a decision which may turn out wrong. Or, to put it another way—faced with a decision, they will do nothing.

What avoiders are looking for from their co-workers are stable, routine assignments which they can do in orderly, precise fashion, sticking exactly to company procedures. If you are direct and systematic in spelling out the rules and explaining the reasons for a particular task, you will give them what they're seeking. By eliminating their need for making decisions, you should solve many of your mutual difficulties. And before you decide that avoiders are totally negative people, remember that in a business world of gossip and carelessness, avoiders follow orders strictly and almost never create conflicts.

## Drug Addicts Where You Work

You may not have realized that heroin addicts who successfully hide their addiction work at all kinds of good jobs—everything from truck driver, construction worker, secretary, baker, mechanic, salesman, and typist to college registrar, bank teller, and plant manager. By keeping their addiction secret, many of them are able to hold their jobs for years and often victimize co-workers in various ways.

A full-scale study by psychologist Stephen Levy of New York's Training for Living Institute revealed that you *cannot* recognize the hard-drug addict by his age or where he lives. Men and women of all ages were discovered to be addicts. Often they lived in suburban "drug-free" communities.

So unsuspecting were most co-workers, that 95 percent of the addicts studied were able to use drugs on the job. Nearby lavatories were very popular places for shooting up. The major danger to fellow workers is the addicts' need for money. To obtain funds to buy their drugs, job-holding addicts pushed drugs at work, stole job supplies from their own and others' work stations, and made off with cash or checks from fellow workers.

If you're being plagued at work by mysterious petty thefts of the kind we've described, addiction may be the explanation. It may now be time for the others in your office and for your company security people to move from "unsuspecting" behavior to actively watching for the physical signs among your co-workers that can help you pinpoint addicts among you.

Also remember: baby-sitting is a job, too. In considering your sitter's reliability, be alert for signs of drug use. Even the so-called soft drugs like marijuana may make a sitter incapable of keeping your child safe.

### Alibi Joe: How Understanding Him Can Save You Grief

"Nobody told me it was due today."
"Sales should have known it couldn't be done."
"Engineering didn't send up enough facts."

These words might have come from Alibi Joe, the employee whose self-confidence exceeds his job competence. Because he exudes so much confidence, Alibi Joe is the guy who often lands a work position that is above his actual ability. Though his co-workers rapidly size him up, he may survive surprisingly long in a large, complex organization.

And despite the fact that he is constantly finding blame elsewhere, Joe is not really interested in "getting" fellow workers. He has only two genuine interests: protecting his own position and preserving his own good opinion of himself. His favorite target is "they" or a whole group such as "sales." Supervisors can solve matters by placing Joe at a level where he can handle the job—but they must also convince him that the new job is compatible with his abilities. If he is not convinced of that, Alibi Joe becomes a dangerous employee. Angry about his "demeaning" new assignment, he will undermine morale by constantly sniping and griping.

### For Men: The Truth About Getting Along with Women Co-Workers

A man who still believes the old-fashioned myths about women workers may find his on-the-job relations with them strained. Before you decide your female co-workers are too touchy, ask yourself if you're creating tension by your unrealistic attitudes.

For years some men have been telling themselves that women work for "pin money" or "to get out of the house." Yet *The Wall Street Journal* reports that *every* survey on why women work produces the same answer. Women work for money just as men do. And women's earnings, like men's earnings, are used to benefit their families. In addition, approximately half of all women workers are the sole or major financial support of their families. Your women co-workers, therefore, will actively resent any intimation that they don't "need" a promotion or don't "need" as good a salary as a man.

Women workers are absent *less* often than comparable men workers, according to U.S. Department of Labor statistics. As for the old cliché, "After a few years their husbands move or the women have babies," turnover among men workers, both blue- and white-collar, is at an all-time high. All employers know they can't depend on male workers to stay forever. Men's and women's actions, then, are the same. Only the reasons they give may differ. Ultimately, the average married woman worker spends twenty-five years on a job; the unmarried woman worker puts in forty-five years compared to the average man's forty-three. The man who hopes to get along with his women co-workers in the new world of the 1970s and 1980s has to recognize these facts and adjust to them.

## Why They're Not Telling You What They're Not Telling You

Lists of do's and don'ts that explain "how to communicate effectively" on your job are everywhere. Yet the what's-going-on-in-this-place knowledge gap remains in most organizations. Why? A recent five-year study of how information moves from a general superintendent to supervisors to workers revealed that some of the problem is caused by laziness or intent to deceive, not by ignorance of "how to communicate." All the supervisors received the same information from their boss at the same meeting. Some took quantities of notes and then held meetings with their subordinates and passed the news on. Others took few notes; some took none. Many never held meetings with any workers; some casually passed on the facts only to special favorites.

A *Personnel Journal* report points out that some people *deliberately* pass on *less* of the story than they receive because they expect to profit in some way from the job confusion that results. They may believe subordinates can't be trusted with the information. Or they feel subordinates might learn enough to ask questions, develop good ideas of their own, or even win a promotion. And for insecure and not overly competent supervisors, "keeping them guessing" can be an attempt to strengthen their own positions.

If you're stuck with a say-little supervisor, you may be able to solve your personal information gap through a friendly co-worker whose boss does send reports down. In struggling to keep track of the job information you need, make an effort to collect news from many sources; you can't depend only on your boss or the co-workers who are supposed to keep you informed about the matter.

## The Memo-Senders

Drowning in paperwork? Though there are endless suggestions on how to lessen the flow, the efficiency approach has limited success because it ignores the hidden human reasons involved. Once you understand what's motivating your fellow employees' paper output, you may be able to give them the recognition or reassurance they're seeking and so reduce their need to put everything into writing.

Even if you can't alter the other person's behavior, understanding it might help you decide which memos and reports really require your attention and which need only a glance. Of course, some reports from co-workers are valuable and necessary. In many other instances, people are writing memos because they want to attract the attention of their boss, protect themselves against any future questions, impress others with their competence, avoid a face-to-face discussion, or as a means of "flexing" their egos and announcing, "I'm in charge of this project." It's also possible that some new kind of elaborate duplicating machine has been installed and is being exuberantly overused so that almost everyone receives a copy of almost everything.

### Deciding About Your New Co-Workers

Joe, Tom, and Nancy are new co-workers. It doesn't take you long to size them up. Tom's not too bright. Nancy's stuck-up. Joe's a nice guy. Months later something happens and you realize with a shock that your estimates of your new co-workers are completely wrong. How could you have been so mistaken?

Basically, say industrial psychologists, there are two traps most of us fall into when we meet someone new. We stereotype and we generalize. We start out with ideas of what kinds of personalities we can expect to encounter in a clerk, trucker, executive, union leader, businessperson, teacher, etc. Then when we meet someone with that job, we're likely to have a prepackaged reaction. Oh, sure, we think we're seeing that individual's personal behavior. But we're really noticing only those traits which fit our stereotype.

We also get ourselves into trouble by generalizing from surroundings. If you first meet people in a formal office setting, you may have one impression of their character. But if you're introduced over a relaxed lunch table, you might have a totally different permanent impression of them. This quickness to generalize goes further. Most people form lasting impressions of others from short introductory conversations. You say something; the other person replies. The answers don't suit you perfectly. And that's it. Based on that short exchange, you form a *permanent* negative opinion of that person. We may even make job trouble for ourselves by judging new co-workers according to generalized facts that don't really apply. For instance, if workers need to be good-natured and accurate with numbers to carry their share of the job, isn't it foolish to react coldly to them because of an irrelevant trait such as weight or their taste in clothes?

# Promotion Strategies 2

Psychologists have discovered that, depending on the social class in which you were raised, you will probably have an active or a passive attitude toward winning a promotion. Blue-collar and lower-middle-class people, the researchers report, tend to believe that things "happen," that life is determined by luck or the "way things break." Upper-middle-class people have usually come to the realization that events can, to some extent, be brought to pass by their own actions or non-actions—which is probably why they are now upper-middle-class! The realization that you and I usually "make our own luck" is absolutely central to understanding "promotion strategies."

Of course, nothing in life is guaranteed. There's the ironic Somerset Maugham tale of the two brothers, one a conscientious clock puncher, the other a heedless wastrel. Despite his lifelong efforts, the hardworking brother never reaps rewards. While he is being done in by a freak accident, the wastrel stumbles into unearned riches. Certainly, things happen illogically—sometimes. But usually we do reap what we sow. Therefore, if you stop thinking of promotion as something to be wished for and instead regard it as an attainable goal to be actively sought, you put the laws of chance to work in your cause.

This chapter examines what you can do to obtain a promotion and then tells how to enjoy it once you have it.

## How to Get Your Superiors' Attention—Favorably!

Since your pay increases, your promotions, and your job security all depend on what others think of you and your work, tactfully making yourself stand out as an individual can be rewarding. Understanding the *real* lines of authority and communication in your department and in your company is an absolute necessity. By paying attention, you should eventually know which people support each other, who are the rivals, who belongs to which clique, and who would have the final say in rewarding you for good job performance.

If you have a job where your work load fluctuates, being honest can be very useful. If you talk up during slack periods and ask if there's anything else that needs doing, your supervisor is more apt to believe you when at other times you say you're overloaded. And the extra tasks you obtain may lead you into new and more responsible assignments.

Sometimes, of course, you can be noticed for the wrong reasons. Gossiping about such things as the "stupidity" of various company policies and taking sides in job disputes involving others are sure ways to bring yourself to everyone's attention as a person who lacks job savvy.

## How to Read
an "Invisible"
Corporate Power
Chart

Every business organization has two power charts—the official one and the real one. The official organization chart is there for anyone to study. The real power chart is invisible, and you can understand it only by persistent observation. Since the invisible power chart affects who gets promotions and raises, who stays and who is elbowed out, it's well worth your while to learn about it. Here are some things to watch for:

1. *Who supplies the reliable information?* A decision-maker or someone having close access to the real decision-maker is the source of such information.

2. *Who has social contacts with top executives?* Social connections may have been achieved through long-standing friendships or through a spouse with good connections or through activities in some political, community, athletic, or religious organization. However gained, they give that person an edge in company power.

3. *Which longtime employees have quietly cornered power by taking on the authority to initial memos or plans?* Even if their initials on the project really mean nothing, by making themselves a part of the chain, these senior employees can delay or kill a project by quietly leaving it on their desks. That's negative power. But it's power.

4. *Which co-workers have relatives or former bosses in the executive hierarchy?* They may have realistic expectations of

promotions that will turn them into powerful people eventually.

5. *Who is currently involved in an office romance?* Someday, it's true, the romance may be over. But at the moment, they're a duo commanding power from two directions in the organization.

Once you understand the real power structure, you'll know how to get results and who is really important to your future with the company.

## Secret Reasons Why People Get Promoted

Most people have the wrong idea about promotions. They think there has to be an opening that needs to be filled. The truth is many women and men are elevated to jobs and titles that are invented for them. Maybe in your own career it would be helpful for you to know the secret reasons why people are promoted. Some are given a lift upward to prevent them from moving elsewhere. This happens when a company is worried about replacements in a tight labor market or about raiding from other businesses. It even happens within an organization. When a competing department within the company shows an interest in X, the department head may give X a better title to prevent a lateral transfer.

How can a person be promoted when there's no real opening? Sometimes the position created is genuine; sometimes it's only token—but the new job brings a better-sounding title and higher salary. (Never turn down a more impressive-sounding title no matter how empty it is. Titles are extremely valuable if ever you go job-hunting.) Then there's a whole labyrinth of in-company "political" reasons which produce status changes. A manager may hurry to advance or recommend an easygoing subordinate to block the rise of someone who may become a dangerous rival. If you make yourself essential to an executive above you, you may be pulled along as the executive moves ahead. If this leader has a yen for empire-building, you're sure to profit. All empire builders must have trusted people they can place in key support offices.

The only problem here is, in order to ride someone's coattails to promotion, you have to choose the right coattail!

## When Someone Else Gets the Promotion

You can stew and complain to your family and friends when someone else gets the promotion you thought belonged to you, or you can do some constructive things that may make you the winner next time. Was the opening in a department other than your own? Maybe your supervisors were too busy with their own problems and never thought to recommend you. Did you ask them to? If the opening was in your own department, *pleasantly* ask your supervisor why you were passed over, and what you need to do to make yourself eligible for the next suitable opening. Then listen—don't argue or offer excuses. Say you'll act on what's been told you and do so.

In his book, *How to Succeed in Company Politics*, Edward J. Hegarty suggests you inquire at this point if you also may draw the supervisor's attention to your strong points. Submit a well-thought-out list of your qualifications. Discuss these points and leave the list with your supervisor. The next time there's an opening, chances are the boss will be aware of you as a candidate.

Says Hegarty: "If you've been tactful and presented a good list, your boss may even feel he owes you something right now for having passed over you, and he may give you a raise, a better title, or some other consideration."

## How the Clothes Women Wear Can Affect Their Chances for Promotion

As the new laws against discrimination encourage women of all ages to seek jobs that lead to promotions and careers, many women may have to rethink their wardrobes. The woman who knows she is a competent employee who should be considered for promotion and increased responsibility has to dress the part.

Many women who have mastered the skills of their jobs have not yet matched their wardrobes to their career expectations. If a woman hopes to be taken seriously at her job, say the personnel experts, she has to realize her clothes help *create* other people's opinion of her. Clothes that are supercasual, kooky, seductive, or mousey drab, for example, all fail to suggest job ability. The key word is *appropriate*. What's right at an advertising agency might be wrong at an insurance firm.

A woman must also understand that nothing is more obsolete than the idea of a career woman as a severe-looking, unattractive female. In today's business world, good-looking clothes and the right makeup and hairstyling are valuable. By choosing an appearance that projects an attractive I-can-do-the-job aura, a woman helps her co-workers and her bosses see her as the capable, promotable person she really is.

### Are You Being Loyal to a Dead-End Job?

Job ruts can be comfortable and practical. They can also be dangerous. In evaluating your position, ask yourself if you're in any of these hazardous job ruts:

1. *Are you working hard for a notoriously low-paying employer?* If you stay long enough, your salary will be out of synchronization with your achievements and responsibilities. You will then have a hard time convincing future employers that you really are competent. The feeling will be, "if you're so good, why were you willing to take such low pay for so long?"

2. *Are you being channeled into a tiny specialty which has*

*little use outside your present company?* You can be the best butter-churn designer in the world, but if your employer stops making churns or refuses to pay you reasonably, where will you find another position? Though the example of butter churns may appear farfetched, this peril exists for any narrow specialty.

3. *Are you a good salesperson who manages to make a living with a so-so item?* You could latch on to a more attractive commodity from which you could get better results with less anxiety.

4. *Are you letting inertia overwhelm you?* Perhaps the people you work for are an unimaginative, just-get-by group that's going nowhere. It's possible they'll change as you've been hoping and you'll get that chance. More likely they'll stay as they are and you'll be stuck. While *too much* job-hopping may weaken your employment record, loyalty to a dead-end job is not sensible either.

### Business Clichés That Could Spell Trouble

Some of the slogans you may hear at work sound more sensible than they really are. If you're not careful, they can keep you from getting ahead. Writing in a leading management publication, Fred Fisher, Vice-President of the National Training and Development Service, points out that comments such as, "Have you checked the company policy on that?" or "Does it square with the organization chart?" can often kill good ideas. Where you have the chance to be flexible about company procedures, you can frequently add to profits or cut costs if you'll stop reacting to new ideas with the above remarks.

When you hear your bosses insisting that "if there's one thing we believe in, it's competition," look around and see if they're talking about healthy competition with your company's business rivals. Or are you in a job where competition has developed *within the company,* and every department is busy using its energy to compete with everyone else for budgets, people, priorities, and even responsibilities?

And if your boss has the attitude "We've got to minimize our risks," realize you're not going to learn very much on this job. A risk-minimizing atmosphere means your boss will expect you and everyone else to forget aggressiveness and stick to conservative company tradition. The boss' next step may be "One mistake and you're out." This, Fisher says, can be one of the most dangerous of business clichés. Mistakes are a cost of doing business in an aggressive outfit and should be brought out in the open and worked on. But in a one-mistake-and-you're-out atmosphere, people naturally will do anything to hide and disguise their errors. So the business loses and no one learns.

## Asking for a Promotion: How Men and Women Differ

Even among married women, half now hold paying jobs. Yet employment experts have noticed that there's a difference between the way most men and women go after promotions and pay increases they think they deserve. A man may take a while collecting his courage, but eventually he'll ask the boss. Most women, however, use an approach based on the belief that "if I'm efficient, I'll be noticed and rewarded."

Probably because of social conditioning, women fail to ask for promotions and pay increments they sincerely believe they've earned. Instead, they toil conscientiously and *wait* for their supervisor to offer a reward. If the boss is a man, he's probably totally unaware of the women's viewpoint. There are always exceptions, but the typical boss-outlook is: "If subordinates don't ask for a promotion, a raise, or other changes, they must be perfectly satisfied, so why put ideas into their heads?" This situation can explode in both management's and women's faces. When a valued woman subordinate suddenly gives notice that she is resigning to take a better job, the boss is frequently shocked; after all, she never intimated to him that she wasn't perfectly content. From the women employees' viewpoint there's no way of toting up all the job heartaches they've endured because they worked silently according to their eventually-I'll-be-rewarded rules—and they never were!

## When You're Promoted Over Your Old Friends

If you've been promoted over your former co-workers, you probably hope to keep your old friendships alive. This will take skill. Besides valuing your old friendships for their own sakes, you will need the goodwill of your friends if you expect them to work well for you.

However, you may find that the buddy-buddy aspects of your relationship, such as eating lunch together every day, will fade. You needn't fear the why-don't-you-eat-with-us?-got-a-swelled-head? reaction. Everybody should understand when you explain that if you don't associate with the other supervisors, you'll never stay in touch with what you're supposed to be doing and won't learn from their experiences.

Don't concentrate so much on comradeship with your old co-workers that you avoid exercising your authority when you have to do so. Your friends will have to realize that they must take all your job orders seriously. If they do not respect the orders you give them, your group's performance will soon suffer. And you'll be heading for failure in your new position.

**Where Enemies
Come From**

When you're promoted to a new position or move on to a new company, you may be astonished to discover you have some ready-made enemies. Some will be people you hardly know. Open rivalry is easy to comprehend, but what causes secret attacks and apparently "pointless" animosity? The better you understand what produces such behavior, the more easily you can locate your secret opponents, anticipate their actions, and cope.

In his American Management Associations' books on business life, Elton T. Reeves points out that ambush hatreds are usually caused by:

1. JEALOUSY   Your enemy would shoot at anyone holding your job. He himself isn't qualified to do the work, yet he'd like to be in your position. Fortunately, this type of jealousy usually leads the attacker into indiscriminate criticism which is clearly untrue.
2. REVENGE   This kind of enemy *is* qualified for your job but was unable to obtain it. By discrediting you, he hopes to push you out and make another try for it.
3. PRIDE   There's the possibility that a person with some authority voted against your getting the job. Now his pride is in-

volved and he's determined to see you fail to vindicate his original judgments against you.

Adding to Reeves's list:

4. THAT'S NOT THE WAY I DID IT!  Your work style is different from that of someone who once held your job or a job similar to yours. Therefore, in that person's eyes, you are wrong or incompetent.

5. YOU'RE NOT GOING TO SHOW ME UP!  When someone takes this attitude, you're obviously competent and a threat to the status quo.

Attacks can take many forms—from withholding information you need, to outright lies and false rumors, to a true account which omits only one significant fact. Sometimes you may succeed by open and direct confrontation which must include documentation for statements you make in rebuttal. Other times you may permanently weaken your enemy by getting others to see him as a sore loser who wants your job. Where you can, turn him into an ally by proving that your success will benefit his job future. The more smoothly you can disarm your opponent, the better. Even when you're the innocent victim, most bosses don't value the employee who turns the work scene into a personality battle.

## When Your Company Wants You to Relocate

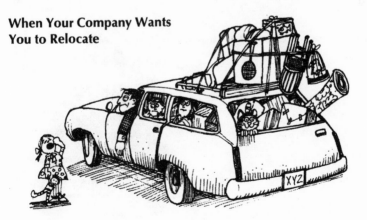

Many married workers turn down a good job they'd really like to have because they know the company will expect frequent relocations. Until 1970 someone who worked for a large corporation might have had to move eleven to fourteen times before reaching a final niche. But since then, the growing resistance of American employees to relocations has forced many corporations to change their moving policies. Therefore, if you've avoided a corporation job because of the prospect of endless transfers, you may want to reconsider. Nowadays, according to Atlas Van Lines' authoritative annual nationwide survey of corporation relocation policies and plans, an employee may only have to move three to four times during a career to reach the desired niche.

The growing employee distaste for being uprooted has also caused companies to greatly increase fringe moving benefits. If you're asked to relocate, you might inquire about the following, which many companies now grant: company-paid expenses for moving an *unlimited* weight of household goods; expenses for moving a second or even a third auto and a boat; financial assistance in disposing of your present residence through payment of all brokerage fees; a guaranteed sale of your old house through company purchase if necessary; and two or more company-paid trips to the new area to househunt. And 12 percent of companies now toss in a tempting new extra—maid service to clean your old home when you leave and/or prepare your new home for your arrival.

## Should You Accept a Promotion?

When the day comes that you're offered an executive position, should you accept? Your family, friends, and inner self may tell you, "Grab it." Yet without being able to put your finger on the reason, you may have doubts about whether you'd enjoy executive work. It's not a matter of brains or ability. Many highly skilled factory, sales, and office workers, and many highly educated scientists, engineers, teachers, etc., have accepted promotions to foreman or office executive and lived *un*happily ever after. Others, of course, accept promotion and live *happily* ever after.

You can judge your own possible reaction to executive life from the following: Johnson O'Connor Foundation researchers, who have tested half a million people for job aptitudes during the last half century, find that to be content as an executive you need (A) an objective, outgoing personality which allows you to *enjoy* dealing with people all day every day; (B) a strong ability to deal with abstract ideas; and (C) a very large vocabulary to aid you in thinking through problems. The researchers warn that there are other personality types who should avoid the executive's desk. Even if they manage the job itself well, success may cost them heavily in emotional and physical health. This was proved by an American Management Associations' survey of three thousand businessmen. Nearly 30 percent of the managers believe that strain, tension, or other job-related factors have adversely affected their health in the past five years. Equally important, 40 percent of all of the middle managers and 52 percent of supervisory-level managers reported that their work is "at best, unsatisfying." According to the Johnson O'Connor Foundation research, these unhappy managers probably do have the brains, but they lack the personality for executive work. Non-executive people are:

1. Happier concentrating on the work itself rather than on the people around them. These kinds of people often find themselves floundering in executive positions. The constant give-and-take with people exhausts them emotionally. They dislike delegating responsibility and want to keep a finger in everything. Because constant human contact wears on them, they are often inaccessible and, though they may work hard at it, they have trouble establishing satisfactory relationships with those they supervise.
2. People with a strong ability to visualize and work with struc-

tures and three-dimensional objects are again working against their own temperaments by taking a desk job where they will "shuffle papers," talk, and deal with abstract ideas all day.

3. People with high creative ability for producing new ideas are often miserably unhappy as executives. Unless they are in sales, advertising, or some other strongly creative area, creative people are restless, bored, and dissatisfied administrators.

# Making Things Break Your Way by Saying It Right 3

"Making things break your way by saying it right" does not involve manipulation. It involves understanding that people are emotional beings, often very insecure and defensive. Though you may mean one thing, their low self-esteem often causes them to read something entirely different into your words. And they then take offense at what you say. You must be constantly alert to this possibility and must stop and clarify when you see the body language signs or hear answers that indicate something is going wrong.

"Saying it right" also involves understanding that people are more highly motivated by their own self-interest than by your convenience. If a request of yours would in some way deliver benefits to them, make clear the benefits instead of putting it solely in terms of "this is what I need."

To communicate effectively you must be everlastingly aware that most people are listening to you through a barrage of noisy internal static. As you speak they are tuning in and out and developing mental pictures that would astonish you. In his excellent book, *Getting Through To People* (Prentice-Hall), industrial psychologist Dr. Jesse S. Nirenberg, a specialist in human communication, gives some interesting examples of how this skews the answers you receive. Here is one:

One person asks another, "Do you think I should ask my father for his advice on this matter?" The second person doesn't know the father and when the word *father* is mentioned the second person sees a harsh, egocentric dictator because of his own experience. The first person, on the other hand, actually has a kindly, helpful father.

The second person is not aware that his own image of his father is prompting his recommendation. He says, "I think you ought to stand on your own two feet, make your own decisions." Now this statement as a generalization has the sound of good sense. However, it might not at all apply in this specific situation and it might very well be motivated by the second person's anger at his father. . . .

In this case the trouble was caused by each person thinking that since they both used the same word, *father*, they both had the same mental image.

In addition to all the emotional factors which cause communication difficulties, there's interference from poor listening habits per se. A University of Minnesota study discovered that, immediately after listening to a talk, people remembered only half of what they'd heard. This listening loss, together with inaccurate listening, constantly embroils people in misunderstandings with customers, co-workers, superiors. Common listening mistakes that you should be aware of in yourself when you're listening to someone, and in others when you are doing the talking, include: Fade Out: tuning out when listening to something dull or difficult. Pretending: going through the motions of looking interested while the mind flits. Prejudiced: the listeners have strong contrary opinions; they are so busy framing a rebuttal that they hear almost nothing of what is being said. Off and On: barely interested in what is being said; every passing sound or person becomes a distraction. Naturally, in all these cases the listener comes away with ideas very different from those which were presented.

If you understand that all these forces—and others which we'll discuss in this section—are interfering with your verbal messages, you can counter by being alert to the telltale signs. You will then be able to make things break your way by saying things intelligently instead of haphazardly.

## Do You Often Talk Yourself into Trouble?

If you frequently find yourself frustrated when discussing a job problem with your boss or co-workers, you may unintentionally be talking yourself into trouble. Do you usually express your ideas in a way that will produce a Yes or No answer? If so, you are setting things up so that you have only a fifty-fifty chance of getting what you want. For example, if you say, "This machine (or schedule) of mine has to be changed or I can't get work done on time," you've boxed yourself in.

If the answer is, "We can't replace the machine (or change your schedule)," what alternatives have you left yourself except a do-or-die fight over your goal? However, if you learn to concentrate on your basic objective and phrase your suggestions so that you give the other person a group of *alternatives,* you raise your chances of success—and you lower the number of head-on confrontations in your work life.

You could have said, "I'm having trouble keeping up my part of the work. There's something wrong with my machine." With this approach you've done two important things. The new way gives the other person a reason for wanting to help you: You've said you can't contribute your share to production. To other people this is a far more important reason for attending to your machine than your flat, personal complaint that you're having a difficult time with it.

Previously, when you said ". . . or I can't get the work done on time," you were delivering a threat, which is always a poor approach. Now you've given the person various alternatives. He can say something like "I'll get maintenance" or "Use Joe's or Mary's machine while they're on vacation and I'll have yours overhauled" or "I'll put in a replacement request." Even if your supervisor says, "Nothing we can do about your problem," you haven't put yourself in a position where you must fight it out to save face. You've also created the impression that you *want* to get your work done, but your equipment (or schedule, or whatever) hinders your performance. Your supervisor will now be more sympathetic if you do not meet your task or job goals.

### Saying Too Much or Too Little

Here are three important rules to remember to keep yourself out of talk-trouble:

1. BE CAREFUL ABOUT HIDDEN MEANINGS  You said, "Sorry, I can't," when Tom suggested eating lunch together. Did you refuse because you don't like eating with Tom? Or is it because you just started a hurried project and you want to gulp your lunch and rush back? A brief word of appropriate explanation often prevents misunderstandings.

2. DON'T VOLUNTEER MORE THAN YOU CAN DELIVER  If you say, "I can do it in a month," when it's really a six-week job, you're going to look like a flop when it does take a normal six weeks. Or when there's a pile of extra work, bravely offering to "get everything done by quitting time" is foolish. Even if you're a whiz and do *almost* all of it, your performance will be disappointing to your supervisors. After all, you told them you would finish it. Although you may be very competent, your promotion and raise potential may suffer if you fre-

quently promise more than is reasonable and then cannot live up to the unrealistic expectations that you created in your supervisor's mind.

3. IF YOU'RE A SUPERVISOR, BE CAREFUL OF WHAT YOU PROMISE When handing out a difficult job, don't try to sugarcoat it by suggesting "good possibilities in the future" if the person does well. He or she is going to translate your vague words into something specific. "The boss said I'm due for a raise or a promotion" is the way it'll be told at home that night. Soon you'll be the only one in your place who doesn't know that you promised Ralph or Mary a raise or a promotion.

## Why People Aren't Reasonable

Salespeople aren't the only ones who have to try to talk others into things. In every job there comes a moment when you want to win another person's cooperation or agreement. Sometimes when you explain your idea, others accept it or give you logical reasons why they're uninterested. At other times, their answers don't seem to make sense. When this happens, you may as well stop talking until you can get an inkling of their *real* reasons. Dr. Jesse S. Nirenberg, consulting industrial psychologist and author of *Getting Through To People,* explains that some of the angriest episodes in business and in families occur when you meet what appears to be irrational opposition. The more patient and logical you are, the less relevant the other person's answers become. This is a sure sign, says Dr. Nirenberg, that your opponent has strong reasons for disagreeing with you but is unwilling to reveal them.

For example, a salesperson finds that a buyer absolutely refuses to place an order no matter how clearly the superiority of the product is demonstrated. If the seller keeps discussing the merits of the product, he will get weaker and weaker excuses from the buyer. But no sale. The truth may be that the buyer is interested in price alone, not durability, and is unwilling to admit it. Consequently, no amount of logic about product quality can move him. Until the seller pauses and tries to discover the buyer's *real* objections, there'll be no sale. Says Dr. Nirenberg, objection-hopping is another sign which should make you pause and consider hidden reasons. If people quickly abandon one objection and repeatedly hop to another when you give sensible responses, you can be sure they're making up excuses as they go along. To ascertain the truth, you'll have to pause and try a new approach.

## How to Deal with Hostile Questions

You've probably noticed that people at work often ask questions in order to get attention, to embarrass you, or one-up you. When you're the target, how do you cope?

Public relations expert Paul R. Edwards suggests that first you learn to recognize the innocent 45 percent of questions that are asked for personal ego reasons. He calls these "message" questions, and they often begin with the person asking, "Don't you think . . . ?" or "Have you considered . . . ?" or "What would happen if . . . ?" The askers are trying to nudge you into agreeing with their views. If possible, do so, and give them the moment of glory they're after. Then move on. If the idea is unacceptable to you, you can still handle it diplomatically if you acknowledge the asker's personal importance by saying something like, "I can tell you've given this a great deal of thought. I share your concern and my thinking is. . . ."

When questions are hostile—and Edwards believes these account for another 45 percent of business questions asked—they often begin with "How come . . . ?" or "Why . . . ?" You can disarm your opponent by quietly admitting a mistake, if there's been one, and saying, "You're right." Since you've reacted without hostility, your questioner has nothing further to say and the incident can be quickly forgotten. Another good approach is to agree and disagree at the same time. You agree with some small part of a remark—for example, "You're right; we should discuss this today"—then you pleasantly present factual evidence or opinion differences for your views. But you never restate your opponent's accusations. That's adding support to his or her side. And it's important to stay in the present; don't be drawn into discussing past history. Says Edwards, "That's the equivalent of walking into a mine field."

As Edwards sees it, only 10 percent of the questions, one in ten, are really attempts to gain information.

## Why Even Good Ideas Are Sometimes Rejected

You've thought of a way to improve efficiency or save money at your job. Now what?

Probably the major mistake people make is to try to sell their new idea to the boss before they find out if the boss realizes the problem exists. Just because you're so aware of the difficulty doesn't mean your supervisor is. What possible interest can he/she have in making the changes you want if he/she doubts there's a trouble situation? Once the boss agrees there's a problem, then you can present your ideas.

Before approaching your supervisor, you should spend time preparing the facts. If you're suggesting a new piece of equipment, then you should have collected brochures and prices, talked to a few knowledgeable people, investigated how this equipment has functioned in similar businesses, and marshalled evidence that the purchase would benefit your concern. If it's a change in business routine, then you should have thought through why the change is needed, how it could be implemented, and how it would affect your co-workers. (Bosses can't accept your ideas for change if they feel the new system would hamper others.)

If, after your best preparation, your idea is rejected, try to analyze why. Sometimes it's because you overlooked a necessary preparatory step. Sometimes the idea wasn't really that good to begin with. And sometimes you will have stumbled onto a better understanding of your local office politics.

**When There's Tension
Between You
and a Co-Worker**

You can feel the silent dislike and tension. Somewhere in the past the relationship between you and a co-worker soured. Yet your own job requires the two of you to discuss matters and occasionally work together. Is there any way to return your relationship to normal business pleasantness? Can you at least relieve the tension so that the two of you can work in calm neutrality?

In a special *Jobmanship* interview, Dr. Jesse S. Nirenberg suggested that you talk with your co-worker about your tension and ask about his/hers. Be careful not to blame. Talk only about your feelings, not about the other person's behavior. Dr. Nirenberg suggested that the dialogue might go something like this:

YOU: I feel a certain tension between us. If we talk about it, maybe we could get rid of the tension and work together pleasantly again. [*Here you're talking about your feelings and getting the other person to talk.*]

OTHER PERSON: We just don't hit it off, so the less we talk about it the better. [*Other person is resisting.*]

YOU: What do you think is wrong between us? Things used to be much better. [*Asking a question to draw the person out.*]

OTHER PERSON: Well, if you really want to know, you try to run the show too much, always talking down to me as if I were a ninny. [*Letting out the anger.*]

YOU: That can be irritating. Could you give me some examples so that I can better understand what you mean? [*Asking for examples when given a generalization about your behavior.*]

If the examples given make you realize that your behavior really is the cause of the tension, thank the other person for helping you and say you're going to try to change. If the examples do not seem to justify the criticism, ask for an explanation—that is, what it is about such behavior that bothers him so much? If the other person can't give any examples, ask him to tell you about it the next time it happens.

Keep in mind the following: (A) ask questions to get the person to talk out reactions, (B) ask for examples, (C) don't blame him even if he blames you, just explore his reactions, and (D) remember, "a soft answer turneth away wrath."

## Avoiding Personality Hassles with People You Work With

There are times when you can't escape—you and a co-worker who have legitimate reasons for disliking each other have to work together on some task. How do you get the job done without a continuing personality hassle? We asked this question of psychologist Dr. John L. Butler, a specialist in industrial problems.

Here is what Dr. Butler suggests. When you have good reasons for being uncomfortable with a particular co-worker and yet have to work closely with that person:

1. Concentrate on your work goals. You won't be insensitive to your co-worker's feelings, but by keeping your mind firmly on the work, you'll be less likely to bog down in personality differences.

2. Spend time at the beginning of the work with both your supervisor and your co-worker. Plan the tasks and responsibilities in advance so that each of you has as much independence and as little overlap as possible in your day-to-day work routine. This will cut down on the daily contacts you'll have with each other.

3. Try putting yourself in your co-worker's shoes and imagine how you and the job look to him. It takes courage to do this, says Dr. Butler: "Many times people find that by trying to understand their co-worker's feelings, they find their approach to their work and to their co-worker changed for the better."

4. If these efforts do not succeed, and you feel you must go to your boss, then be careful not to downgrade the other employee as a person. Dr. Butler adds that of course you'll talk the matter over with your boss in private. It's also useful to have more than one alternative solution ready to suggest. With your boss, examine the problems by concentrating on how the co-worker and you differ in work habits, style, and approach to the job. Remember, your private discomfort is more important to you than to your supervisor. To enlist the supervisor's active cooperation, you'll need to emphasize the fact that you are interested in getting the job done well and that good job results will require a compatible team.

And on those days when you most feel the tension between you, remember that you don't have to argue everything out. You can doubtless perform the job together without agreeing on every single point!

### Keeping Personal Anger Out of Job Disagreements

Next time you realize battlelines are being drawn between you and a co-worker, ask yourself whether you're disagreeing over (A) facts, (B) methods, or (C) goals. Many tense situations develop needlessly because one of you doesn't have all the required information. Before letting your temper rise or before you both coldly turn away from each other, try saying, "Let's check and see if we have the *same* facts." Then compare them.

Warren H. Schmidt, a noted behavioral science expert and consultant to many industries, explains that people in a job conflict often don't realize that they agree completely on major points and it's only details that separate them. Angry feelings can be neutralized if, after you've checked the facts, you're able to say, "We seem to agree on what the problem is. And we agree on what we'd like to accomplish. It's just the method of getting there that we need to talk about." When it's your goals and those of the other person that conflict, try to discover *why* you've come to different conclusions. Again, do you have different information? Or is it because one of you had some experience that makes you judge the facts differently?

Let's say, for example, that you've both heard another employee promise to take care of an important matter on time. Yet you and a co-worker are now disagreeing about what to do next. Why? Maybe one of you has faith that the person can be depended on to keep his word, while the other has had unfortunate experiences with him in the past and doesn't believe he is trustworthy.

You can also save wear and tear on your emotions by realizing that some job disagreements are the result of your job assignment and have nothing personal in them. For example, if you are the union representative, naturally you and the company representative are frequently going to disagree. But it's not a necessary part of your work to allow personal antagonisms to develop and thereby complicate your business discussions. In fact, you will ultimately accomplish far more for your side if you will create an atmosphere which encourages compromises on the part of your opponent. You can create this atmosphere by keeping personal anger out of your job disagreements.

### Why Do You Get So Little Cooperation?

Do you ever wonder why you find it hard to get cooperation from other people in your company? Without realizing it, you may have been frustrating them! Suppose someone stops to ask you how to handle a certain job situation. Although you're outwardly polite, you may believe he's trying to take advantage of your hard-earned experience, and so you tell him as little as possible. Or over lunch a co-worker in a similar job suggests how you might resolve a work problem. You quickly turn off his attempt to act like a "big shot" and give you advice. If you consistently react in these ways, others may see you as a cold, even hostile, person and respond to you accordingly.

Though the business world is certainly not a land of undiluted kindness, you do have to be flexible in judging your co-workers' motives. Not everyone is out to get you. Many people who want to talk about their new ideas are simply attempting to share their excitement at having found a better way to do something. If you'd encourage them in their enthusiasm, they'd not only cooperate, they'd pass on information you might find useful in your own job. And being too shrewd to allow anyone "to pick your brains" means that when you need answers, you're left wondering, "Why won't anyone cooperate?"

Your ideas about "character" can also unintentionally separate you from others. If you believe that asking for or accepting help at work marks a person as weak or incompetent, your contempt for people who accept aid will follow. Because of your attitude, you may find yourself locked into an isolated position and left to do everything by yourself.

Your behavior during inevitable job crises can be another cause of antagonism toward you. If you withhold facts and assistance that could ease the other person through a rough work situation, you may make your own performance look fine by contrast. But word gets around. What are you going to do on the day *you* need emergency backup and cooperation?

## Winning an Argument

Winning an argument at work can sometimes backfire—you have the satisfaction of winning but you also have a brand-new enemy. In all probability, you could have made your point and ended the matter easily and pleasantly if you hadn't pushed the other person into disliking you. As you talked, every time you said something like "That's not true" or "I absolutely don't agree" or "You're wrong about that," you were emphasizing the antagonism between you. You were, in effect, telling the other person, "You don't know what's going on," which is a guaranteed way to maye anyone furious!

Had you, instead, forced yourself to be pleasant and then picked out some points on which you and your opponent *did* agree, the outcome might have been decidedly different. You might have said, "Yes, I see you're right on this point" and "Yes, I agree about that. But I think in this instance it has to be done another way." By acknowledging that the other person is right in some things he says or does, you make it easier for him to admit that you, too, might be correct about a few things.

In order to catch ideas you do agree with, you have to *listen* when your opponent talks. Most people are so busy thinking about their next answer that they don't really hear what the other person is saying. If you do listen, you may even discover the whole battle is based on some innocent misunderstanding, or that the two of you really aren't so very far apart in your views.

**Asking for That Raise**

To increase your chances for success, try to look at yourself, your employer, and your bargaining position as the boss will. *Automation*, a business-engineering publication, recently produced a major report on salaries. Its conclusions would apply to anyone in any job. Here are some things to consider:

1. ARE YOU REALLY WORTH A RAISE? Face the fact that a particular job is worth only so much to an employer. Have you already reached the maximum salary for that work? "Routine paper-shuffling simply does not command the salary paid for stomach-churning duties on the firing line."

2. HOW'S BUSINESS, AND HAS YOUR COMPANY BEEN GROWING? If the answer is, "Business is great and we have been growing," it's sensible for you to expect to share the success. But many people ignore their employer's financial condition and plunge

ahead with their demands. If the company is having a rough time or has hit a stagnant period, is it realistic for you to expect your personal income to be boosted?

3. HAVE YOUR DUTIES AND RESPONSIBILITIES INCREASED SINCE YOUR LAST RAISE? Any significant added duty is a specific extra contribution you can mention when asking for a raise.

4. HAS YOUR EMPLOYER FALLEN INTO THE CARELESS HABIT OF EX-PLOITING WILLING, PRODUCTIVE EMPLOYEES (YOU, FOR INSTANCE) AND HANDING OUT EQUAL PAY FOR DISTINCTLY UNEQUAL PER-FORMANCE? If so, you may have a strong case if you handle it properly. In a quiet talk with the boss, present yourself "as the earnest employee simply making a reasonable inquiry." Have a well-thought-out list of your contributions to the organization and put forth your case pleasantly. Do not appear indignant. And never issue threats or ultimatums—they may turn the discussion away from salary and direct it towards talk of a mutually agreeable termination date.

## When Your Boss Won't Give You a Raise

What can you do if the boss says "No" when you ask for a raise? If you really believe you must have more money to stay with the job, then you may want to make the boss aware of your feelings.

In an exclusive *Jobmanship* interview, Dr. Ernest Dichter, the internationally recognized "father of motivational research," set up some useful guidelines. Says he, be careful not to put the boss in a defensive position. Telling supervisors that you realize they might have given you a raise anyway but with their busy schedule it's possible they haven't had time to arrange it, would be an appropriate opening. Avoid threats like "Either I get the raise, or. . . ." Threatening the boss is never a good approach. It creates a mood of antagonism in a situation where you need a mood of cooperation. Worse yet, if the supervisors must refuse your request, your threats will leave them feeling they have a dissatisfied employee. They may then wonder if your dissatisfaction will cause you to hold back on a full day's work. Therefore, if you receive a turndown, be sure your supervisor knows that you plan to continue working as hard as ever.

Indicating a few weeks in advance that you'll be asking for a raise is a valuable technique. For the average boss, saying "No" to an honest request for better wages is never pleasant. "Giving the boss advance notice," explains Dr. Dichter," offers you a better chance. Even if management still has to refuse, they will have thought the matter out, will feel more comfortable with you, and may give you a raise as soon as they can."

# Shining Up Your Image 4

"Shining Up Your Image" may sound like a public relations hype to you. And that may seem phony. But the fact is, you *must* shine up your image. You have no choice and there's nothing phony about doing so.

Whether you like it or not, you already possess an on-the-job image. Your co-workers see you as a certain kind of person. Your boss believes he/she can predict how you're likely to perform. These people's views of you often control the atmosphere of your every workday and your promotion progress because their image of you becomes a self-fulfilling prophecy.

You yourself have undoubtedly seen how image produces a self-fulfilling prophecy when it operates for or against others. You probably started noticing it subconsciously way back in first grade. It went right on flourishing before your eyes all the way through every year of your school education. There were young-sters in your classes who only had to err slightly and the teacher came down on them "like a ton of bricks." Others could do the same thing, or worse, and all the teacher did was mildly reproach them. Why the difference? The first boys and girls had developed an image with the teachers as "troublemakers." Because a teacher knew *beforehand* that they "made trouble," that's how she interpreted their behavior. The same actions by girls and boys who had reputations as "nice children" were seen differently. These youngsters' shiny images protected them and eased their way in every situation.

At work you've surely noticed the same dual response. Some people are marked "OK," others are marked "victims." People don't mimic, backstab, or gossip about the OK people, who project good-guy and good-gal images. The "victims," however, are fair game for all kinds of casual verbal abuse, though their behavior often is really no different from the behavior of the OK people. The difference between the two groups lies in the eyes of the viewers.

In addition to a job-social image, each person projects a job-capability image. Those who make the right impression have their suggestions, plans, and requisitions treated seriously. If they speak at a meeting, others take up their comments and respectfully discuss them. The people who have projected the wrong job-capability image find that others' negative expectations constantly work against them. Their comments at meetings are shrugged off, regardless of merit. Their job successes are glossed over. In every way, others' attitudes toward them demean and sap their self-confidence.

If you know that you are already handicapped by a poor job image, it's worthwhile considering a job change so you can start afresh. Even if you were to change your behavior drastically at your present job, it's almost impossible to get your co-workers to rethink their current opinion of you. Human nature just doesn't work that way.

But for the average person, the suggestions in this chapter can be very helpful. They can move you from a reasonably satisfactory to a shiny image. With your shiny glow, people will expect you to be competent at your work, OK socially, and altogether a winner.

## "Meetingship": How to Make Yourself Look Good at a Meeting

There are so many ways to inadvertently make yourself look bad at a meeting that you can often look good simply by avoiding the traps. A department, sales, shop, group, or union meeting all offer you an opportunity either to impress others with your ability or to unintentionally attract unanimous disapproval.

For best results, think and speak positively. Forget the hatchet work; let someone else make that mistake. If you feel you must oppose an idea, don't attack it directly. Instead, support another viewpoint. In other words, don't be *against* another person's idea; be *for* another suggestion. This is necessary because no matter how logical an attack may be, it conveys a negative and obstructionist image of you. And every time you open your mouth at a meeting, remember that other people sitting there probably feel as vulnerable as you do. Even mild criticism of someone else's performance, ideas, or views invariably earns you the enmity of the one criticized. If you want to offer a better idea, try saving the previous speakers' egos by building your idea on theirs and saying something like "What's been said is good, but could we also consider . . . ?"

Management consultant Martin Smith suggests that when you

yourself are the target of critical comments at a meeting, you act calmly no matter how upset you may actually feel. If you become emotional, people may think the negative comments are justified. Also, Smith adds, never say, "You're wrong." Instead, concentrate on the positive. Try, "I see what you mean but there are facts that you may not be aware of." (Here you're offering a positive response by citing the existence of other facts.) "Once you see the whole picture, you may change your mind." (You're not attacking. You're saying you're sure your opponent is a rational person who will come to a different conclusion when he/she "knows all the facts.")

With this approach you've put your opponents on the defensive. Though your every word has been positive, you've made it seem they are irresponsible, that they spoke up without checking into all the facts. If they persist in the attack now, they're going to look emotional and irresponsibly disinterested in the truth, while you will look calm, organized, and in command.

## Who Is Keeping You in the Background at Meetings?

You may be able to do something about job meetings where too much time is spent accomplishing too little and where you and your projects never seem to receive attention. At your next meeting, watch and see who is pulling the meeting out of shape and pushing you into the shadows by playing the "hidden decision" and "hidden agenda" games.

According to management expert Richard C. Grote, hidden decisions are made regularly at meetings. Says Mr. Grote: When someone announces, "Let's examine the such-and-such problem . . ." and instantly begins a long discussion, he is single-handedly making a common kind of hidden decision that determines the thrust of the entire meeting. The meeting—and you—may also suffer when someone who is personally unpopular offers a good suggestion that supports your idea. The group may use the "hidden decision" to ignore him, and quickly dismiss his useful comments. And if a popular person's ideas are always discussed in time-consuming detail, whether the ideas are good or bad, you are all victims of still another kind of hidden decision.

The "hidden agenda" game can be started for someone's personal goals. For example, John Doe may take up considerable time urging that a new project of doubtful value be considered. "The company's welfare" will be John's expressed purpose, but the new project's advantages to John's own career advancement will be the "hidden agenda" part of his proposal.

Infighting can also produce a time-consuming hidden agenda which robs you of opportunities to put forth your proposals. People involved in infighting may seem to be talking about the meeting's topics. But they are really using the topics to display themselves and/or put one another down.

People who successfully influence your meetings with these games may be playing their roles unconsciously. Or they may be well aware of what they're doing. Either way, once you catch on, you can, either as a group member or as a leader, subtly help control them and capture for yourself your share of time in the spotlight.

**Should You
Confide in
Co-Workers?**

It all depends. There are some things you might want to tell your boss. Other things you'd be wise to keep to yourself even if you almost choke on them.

Trying to develop a special relationship with your boss by acting as a personal listening post usually fails disastrously. Telling supervisors what "people are saying" about them will definitely spotlight you as a special person—a gossip and troublemaker. But if a jealous co-worker is circulating serious lies about you, you might quietly confide in your boss. No histrionics—just a calm passing on of information. The people in charge may do nothing about situations like this when they learn of them, but their knowledge will protect you when the false rumbles reach their ears.

Personal troubles are a whole category of their own. If there's serious illness in your family, it may be wise to let people know.

You may think you're behaving normally at work despite your worries, but others may notice erratic actions. If they understand the cause, they'll be more willing to overlook occasional lapses. However, when you're beset by marital and romantic difficulties or embarrassing legal, monetary, and similar personal dilemmas, don't be too quick to let it all hang out. The one person you're telling it to may be all right. But what about this person's other good friends who will soon be hearing the story? And the people after that? Why compound your difficulties by tarnishing your job image? Then you'll have two problems instead of one.

## When They Change Your Job Duties

Almost everyone reacts with anxiety and perhaps even hostility when he/she first hears, "There're going to be changes made around here." The changes could involve new machines or new organizational routines or both. Naturally your first thought is, "How will it affect me and my job?" Since you can't stop the change, learn some protective actions to make things easier for yourself.

To begin, if at all possible, try to obtain some straight answers from your supervisor. You'll have saved yourself quantities of anxiety if the answer is, "We're going to retrain you to work the new machines. You won't have any problems learning."

Another major worry: How will the changeover affect your seniority if new people are hired who already know the machines? Ask, instead of blindly worrying. Nowadays, even where no union exists, management is often sufficiently enlightened to develop changeover plans that safeguard the current workers. When exactly will the changes be made? What's the benefit of the new system or equipment? The answers may please you. Perhaps you've been struggling for years with problems that the new equipment will eliminate.

But be careful about whom you ask and whom you listen to. Learn to distinguish between the meaningless rumors that circulate during every changeover and the facts given by management.

Guard against making the changeover difficult for yourself because of negative thinking. Don't prejudge the new methods, routines, or tools as bad. Comments like, "That new system will make things more complicated and slower instead of faster" or "Those new machines have so many bugs they're worthless" only make it harder for you to learn.

Realize that even with a good attitude, it will take you some time to become accustomed to new ways and new tools. But with a cooperative viewpoint, you'll hurry the day when the new and the strange begin to feel like the comfortable and the familiar.

## How to Break In Fast When You Switch Careers

Pro football players go from sports into business. Former President Harry Truman went from storekeeping to politics. And millions of other Amercans every year switch from one kind of work to a totally different kind.

If you're planning a change, don't expect your new boss to work as hard breaking you in and "holding your hand" as your first boss did when you were a youngster fresh out of school. Even though you may be a novice at this kind of work, the boss and your new co-workers expect you to know about the job and the business world. You can help yourself by learning the vocabulary of your new occupation as quickly as possible. If you don't recognize the slang name for a tool or the business shortcut words of your new job, others will see you as an inefficient outsider.

In dealing with your new co-workers and new boss, you can probably help yourself by remembering what you did at your last job that bothered people. Were you always the one who was so "overworked" (disorganized?) that you couldn't keep up? Whatever your biggest failing was elsewhere, beware of it in the new occupation. If it bothered others before, it will annoy your new co-workers also.

## Which People Can You Trust?

Once you understand your co-workers' personalities, you're better able to decide who can be trusted. Who is going to be honest with you, and who's likely to make trouble for you behind your back?

According to psychiatrist Anslie Meares, when you realize that one co-worker is very insecure and another is always concerned with doing things "just so," you have found two people who *can* be trusted. The insecure person is too terrified of the possible result of dishonesty to take any risks. And the just-so, obsessive person can not live with the anxiety that results from deceptive behavior. So they stay honest!

Keep away, though, from the very suspicious person. Overly suspicious men and women have a confused idea of what is really going on. Fellow workers who are always talking about how others are "taking advantage" of them fall into this category. These people are unreliable, not because they may deliberately mislead you, but because their own mental confusion gives them mistaken ideas of what is happening around them.

You should also avoid the psychopath. You can recognize psychopaths, says Dr. Meares, by their records of dishonesty, lack of anxiety, and cold absence of concern for others. Giving the psychopath another chance after you catch one of them engaged in some connivery is useless, says Dr. Meares. They have defective consciences and do not learn from experience.

## Hidden Causes: Why Are You Late for Work So Often?

You may be a good worker but you'll eventually strain your boss' patience if you are frequently late. When your lateness is caused by an emergency or serious family illness, everyone understands. But if you are chronically unable to arrive on time, you may be able to help yourself. Decide which of the following hidden reasons apply to you. Once you do understand the *real* reasons, you'll be in a better position to help yourself.

1. Perhaps you need a new job. You may find it hard to arrive on time because you dread facing another workday. You may have outgrown your job or may find it too full of tension. Or is it a co-worker who wears you out? A job with different conditions could change your daily outlook and your ability to be prompt.

2. Perhaps you need to develop a better personal schedule, one that faces the facts. Many people honestly believe it when they tell you, "It takes me only half an hour in the morning to dress and eat." Some people do manage in half an hour but many others really require forty minutes or an hour or more. Till they face the truth about their own tempo and set the alarm clock accordingly, they'll continue to be late. Also, in examining your schedule, consider the possibility that you're trying to accomplish too much in the morning. You may have

developed the habit of doing "just one more little thing before I leave for work."

3. Perhaps you are still fighting long-gone battles. Psychologists say that much chronic lateness is due to resentment which may have begun with parents or some person who currently controls your life and which now may be turned toward all authority. Since the time clock represents authority, you may find it hard to conform to it. Other times lateness is simply a result of bad habits. Perhaps your parents were constantly hurrying you to school and you fell into a pattern of resisting. Or maybe it was something as simple as being called a "slow-poke" as a child and learning to believe it and to act accordingly.

## When You Play Hooky from Work

Be careful how you stretch the truth about job absences. In a union-management case which was brought before the American Arbitration Association, a worker (we'll call him Pete Jones) had taken a three-day funeral leave. When Pete returned to work and filled out the company form, he claimed the deceased as his brother. The next day someone informed the personnel director that the deceased had been Pete's cousin, not his brother.

The company fired Pete for falsifying company records. The union went to his aid, insisting that the company hadn't lost any money because the lie had been discovered before salary for the absences were paid. The union also declared that Pete had learned his lesson and wouldn't try it again. The arbitrator, however, decided that Pete Jones was fired for good! Said he, "Falsification of company records is a very serious offense which does not call for progressive discipline."

The distinguished labor-management publication *Employee Relations In Action* commented, "Most arbitrators would agree with this award, except perhaps in the case of a real old-timer who had been with the company many years and had a superior work record."

## Don't Abuse Your Unemployment Benefits

Can you deliberately get yourself fired in order to collect unemployment benefits? A worker in South Dakota tried it and ended up with a legal case. "The state owes me my unemployment compensation," the worker insisted. "I was fired for being incompetent."

His former employer fought the worker's claim. The employer said, "This man worked well for six months. Then suddenly he began coming in unshaved, sloppy, and late. His attitude became unpleasant and he began to make many mistakes on his job. Also, his supervisor actually heard him telling a co-worker, 'I'm going to make the company fire me so I can collect unemployment.'"

The South Dakota Commission decided against the worker (S.D. Comm. Dec. #2073–C–250). It was not proper, the commission ruled, for the worker to act in such a way as to cause his employer to discharge him. The worker therefore was not eligible and could not collect unemployment-insurance benefits.

## Your Weight and Your Career

Did you know that being overweight can lower your chances for (A) getting a job, (B) winning promotion if you already have a job, and (C) keeping your job? One national weight control plan (Diet Workshop) found that one out of three members reported their weight caused job-hunting and job-retention problems. An international recruiting firm puts it clearly: "Obesity has damaged careers."

Excess weight can cost an executive $10,000 a year in salary, reports another personnel agency which analyzed fifty thousand executive positions it had filled. The overweight executive finds it harder to win promotion or to land the better, higher-paying assignment. "Thinness is taken as an indication of self-discipline," says the Diamond Shamrock Corporation.

In other cases, factory and office workers have been told point blank, "Your only fault as an employee is your weight. No chance of promotion." Some companies have no clear policy on the subject. Others which fear equal-employment-opportunity suits insist they have no policy; yet in hiring and in promotion, prejudice against overweight people is often evident. Still other companies have had openly stated policies. A California utility company gave overweight employees six months to reduce or to face unemployment. An Ohio utility company has refused applicants who are 20 percent or more overweight. "Higher disability rate," they explain. One large southwestern city has been even stricter. They've refused to hire anyone who is more than 15 percent overweight. Maybe these facts will give you the diet willpower you've been searching for.

## The Boss–Secretary Romance

When the young, blonde authoress of the book, *How to Make It in a Man's World*, writes about the boss-secretary relationship, you have to believe she knows the facts of today's business world. Letty Cottin Pogrebin, whose book is a guide to making it in the man's world of jobs, started as a secretary and became an outstandingly successful executive while still in her twenties. A former New York-based book publicist, she is credited with guiding both *Sex and the Single Girl* and *Valley of the Dolls* to their great prominence. Yet she is firmly against boss-secretary romances. From every angle, she says, they're a serious practical mistake.

As Mrs. Pogrebin explains it, a boss who has an efficient secretary may want to think twice before romancing her. He has to realize that as soon as the infatuation cools, the resulting office tension usually pushes the girl into abrupt unemployment. The boss is then left alone to make the unpleasant discovery that romance is only romance, but an efficient secretary is hard to replace.

Mrs. Pogrebin's knowledgeable estimate is that only "one girl in 10,000 finagles a better job as the result of an office affair" and "perhaps one girl in fifty thousand lands the boss as a husband. . . . The worst tales of woe," she concludes, "have been told me by businesswomen who tried to buck the statistics."

# Reading the Boss' Mind   5

It's 10:20 A.M. Steve Birkos and Linda Rawson pass each other in the hallway near the boss's door. "What kind of mood is he in today?" Linda asks.

Steve grimaces.

"That bad, huh?" says Linda. "I was going to talk to him about the McCoy situation. I guess I'll wait."

"I'd keep out of his way altogether," says Steve.

"You bet," Linda replies, and they both take off.

Almost everything the average person knows about how to cope with the boss's moods, whims, eccentricities, habits, and personality are summed up in these trite remarks by Linda and Steve. Industrial psychologists have discovered that, like Steve and Linda, almost everybody has a passive attitude toward *creating* the boss's reactions because they see the boss as a kind of god. Since the boss really does have so much control over people's daily activities, job future, income, and quality of their daily life, people allow fear to dominate their boss-relationship. Added to this fear are all the psychological inhibitions people acquired in childhood about dealing with those in authority. In a child's eyes, parents, teachers, and other adults represent power and authority. They really can withhold desired privileges and objects, inflict corporal punishment, and altogether control the child's life.

Most women and men, say the industrial psychologists, transfer to their bosses the same combination of dependency and fear that they had for the authority figures of their childhood. As a result of this unchanged childish attitude toward authority, they lose sight of the fact that the boss is just another adult like themselves—not a god, but a plain human being with all the foibles, weaknesses, fears, problems, and other human traits.

Once you do stop seeing the boss as an all-powerful, superperson, you are able to increase your leverage with him or her enormously. Instead of simply waiting for the daily mood report, you study the boss' personality as you would that of any friend, customer, or family member. You learn the "red flag" areas. You come to understand the boss' motivations, why the boss does the things he/she does. In understanding the "why," you gain the ability to foresee and exercise some control over the situation so that you can often produce in your boss a good mood toward yourself that induces cooperation.

When the boss talks, you learn to listen between the lines to the real meanings; then, armed with this knowledge, you know what to do to please. You learn to read body language so that, again, you can accurately interpret the boss' real messages.

This section gives you information you need to start dealing with your boss as an understandable human being instead of an enigma.

### Should You Tell the Boss the Truth?

Businesspersons like to talk about how "we're all part of the team," and many bosses add, "I don't want people 'yessing' me all day. I want the truth." But do they? If you learn to be careful about how and when you offer a "no," you may be able to block decisions that do seem wrong to you and possibly aid some of your own projects. The last thing you want is a reputation as a crank and an obstructionist. So:

1. Study your boss and learn the difference between a real request for your views and meaningless talk. Many bosses will ask your opinion about some matter after they've made a firm decision about it. Don't waste a "no" here. If you listen carefully, you'll eventually catch on to your boss' way of asking a question to which he truly wants an answer.

2. Learn also to distinguish between a *real* question and the times your boss is using you as a passive wall to bounce ideas against. At those times, bosses themselves don't clearly know what they want or what the problem is. Neither do they want your ideas on the matter. They just want to talk out loud about it a little.

3. Realize that bosses are human. When the time arrives for a genuine discussion, avoid counterproposals in front of others. If you disagree before a group, you put supervisors in a position where they may have to ignore you in order to maintain their own standing.

4. When you do disagree, use all the tact you can. Telling the boss, "You're overlooked this . . ." or "I guess you never heard

of . . ." or "We tried it before . . ." is sure to produce hostility. Using phrases such as "Might it be useful to find out . . . ?" or "You're right, something ought to be done . . ." or "Should we consider . . . ?" is a much more practical way to tell the boss the truth.

## Deciphering the Boss' Hidden Messages

Bosses often make a point of telling you, "I'd like complete frankness between us at all times." Yet they probably don't mean it. More likely, frankness seems to them to be a potential threat and that's why they have brought it up in conversation with you. You might be safe in assuming that what they really mean is, "Don't tell me anything I don't want to hear."

Another time, after you ask for some change in your routine, you may be told, "Well, I'll try and see what I can do for you." As soon as you hear "try," you've been tipped off that your supervisors are not going to overexert themselves on this matter, and chances are the final answer will be, "We tried, but it didn't work out."

Or you offer a new idea. If your boss replies that it seems to have merit, but adds, "Let me sleep on it" or "I'd like to give it a little more thought," don't come to work the next day expecting a final decision. The "Let me sleep on it" approach informs you that your idea may be satisfactory, but it really doesn't seem very urgent to your boss.

These and other explanations appear in a book, *Metatalk: Guide to Hidden Meanings in Conversation* (Trident Press), written jointly by a lawyer, Gerard I. Nierenberg, and a business consultant, Henry Calero, who are nationally recognized leaders in the art of business negotiation. The authors also warn against being taken in by supervisors who seem to soft-pedal their importance with phrases such as, "May I make a small suggestion?" or "If I may offer a new approach. . . ." When they go to that much trouble to be modest about their advice, it's usually not a "suggestion" and they don't think it's a "small" idea. What they really mean is, "Do it this way."

## Understanding Body Language

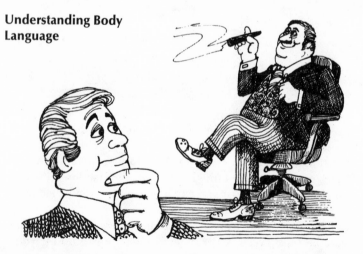

You can often find out what your boss, co-workers, or customer is thinking by observing body actions. Though many people are experienced in disguising their facial expressions, few can camouflage their instinctive gestures. Body language is a growing science that's being studied by academic specialists. When you "have a feeling" the other person really means something different from what he's saying, you're subconsciously reacting to what his gestures say. Without realizing it, you've been interpreting body language.

By developing the ability to consciously watch for messages, you'll be better able accurately to understand what others are telling you. You can start with the following, which are often true (nothing about human nature is ever 100 percent true).

When the person you're talking to reaches up and clasps his hands together on the back of his neck and keeps them there, he's feeling unsure of himself at the moment. By using his hands to reinforce his spinal column, he's subconsciously trying to strengthen himself.

The person who leans forward and places his fingertips together in an arc in front of him is bodily telling you he feels very sure of himself. That finger arc—or "church steeple"—is saying, "You'll have a hard time persuading me to change my mind."

Someone who leans abruptly back is plainly informing you that you're being too aggressive. When you're trying to sell someone an idea and he pauses, looks up, and perhaps blinks rapidly, it's usually a clear sign he's considering your suggestion seriously. Often it means he's accepted your major idea and is now thinking about details.

One body language expert, Merlyn Cundiff, distinguishes between two different meanings that folded arms convey. Many people have heard that folded arms indicate hostility, coupled with a closed mind. In her book, *Kinesics* (Parker Pub. Co. Inc.), Ms. Cundiff explains that this interpretation is true when arms are folded high and firm on the chest. However, when you see arms folded gently and loosely across the lower part of the body, all is well. This often indicates relaxation and a good mood.

What does your body language tell about you?

### Coping with the Boss' Criticism

Criticism from the boss hurts. How you react can determine whether you'll grow or stagnate in your company. Most people's natural reaction is to defend themselves and mentally "prove" to themselves that the boss was wrong or unreasonable. Yet you'll do yourself and your career more good if, after the first shock, you quietly examine the situation honestly. Your supervisor's words may be truer or more revealing than they seemed at first. Do you fall into any of these traps?

1. You mull over criticisms, convincing yourself that the boss probably didn't mean what was said because he/she was just "letting off steam" or didn't know all the facts. So there's no need for you to make any changes in your job behavior.

2. You tend to see yourself as a victim. Victims comfort themselves by muttering, "Why doesn't he make up his mind about what he wants?" or "Doesn't she know it can't be done that way?" or "Why does he want everything done yesterday?" Victims find this rationalization easier than learning to think ahead and anticipate or plan for job and boss needs.

3. You consistently ignore criticism which reflects your boss' basic personality and style. Instead of learning from these sessions, you go on in your own way. For example, though your boss is a hard-driving, short-fused supervisor, you're rarely careful about promises or commitments you make to co-workers, customers, or suppliers. When your promises aren't kept, your

kind of boss is quick to explode and bawl you out. By taking these explosions seriously and making promises you can keep, you'll alter your career potential. Where the boss' criticisms follow a pattern, instead of just living with them, analyze the pattern. Then aid yourself by eliminating from your work habits the actions that trigger the outbursts.

## Are You Having Trouble with Your New Boss?

You may have a new job and a new boss or the same old job with a new boss over you. Whichever it is, you may realize that tensions are developing between you and your new supervisor. Have you considered the possibility that you yourself may be creating the unpleasantness? Are you assuming that everything on the job should be done in the way *you* are used to?

Industrial psychologists have discovered that all of us have our own personal mind-picture of what a boss is and how a boss should behave. As a result, people often create boss troubles for themselves by failing to adjust to the new boss' methods. Instead they wait impatiently for the boss to "catch on" and adjust his/her behavior! People like this will often think and talk about "how things were with my other boss" instead of learning to work with the new one. Another of their favorite comments is, "If the boss would only change."

You can also provoke "new-boss trouble" for yourself by giving up and deciding that you and the new boss will never be happy together. But by keeping an open mind, you give the new boss time to discover your capabilities while you learn his/her wants and style. This eventually could lead to a good working relationship between you.

### The Person Who Is
### After Your Job

Somehow another worker and you seem to have become rivals for the boss' approval. It's not a healthy sales-total kind of rivalry but a personal competition where your job seems to be at stake. Each day the two of you are busy creating opportunities to criticize each other's work while you try to make yourself look good. Management consultants agree that this kind of in-company competition is always a sign that an unsatisfactory executive is in charge.

Many executives instigate rivalries in their departments in the mistaken belief that pitting one person against the other will force each into top performance and the better one will triumph. What actually happens is that the effectiveness of both employees involved is damaged. And it's the better politician, not necessarily the better employee, who usually wins. While the rivals are so busy protecting their jobs by plotting strategy against each other, they have little time or energy left to think about the work itself. Their output and the company suffer. When other competent people in the department lose patience with the conniving ones and quit, the organization suffers again.

Though infighting doesn't always begin with management, it does need management's encouragement to continue. When this kind of rivalry flourishes in your place of work, you should suspect that management is fanning it. Whether or not you want to stay with this kind of supervisor is something for you to consider.

## Bosses Who Smother

Do you have the nagging feeling that your supervisor is not allowing you to develop the decision-making ability you must have for job success? If so, you may have a "smother-type" boss.

It's not very hard to recognize smother-type supervisors once you know what to look for. Usually they are egocentric and domineering. You'll find that they try to keep strict, detailed control over their area, and they have subordinates representing various levels of responsibility all reporting directly to them. You can also recognize the bosses who smother by their wide mood swings, which everyone under them soon learns to watch for. Often they assign responsibilities on impulse instead of logically deciding whose job it should be. Yet they never truly delegate any of their authority.

In his book, *Interpreting Executive Behavior*, George S. Swope explains that subordinates working for a boss with this kind of personality "become incapable of making an independent decision." Obviously, staying too long with a smother-boss is dangerous to your career future.

## If Your Boss Owns a Small Business

Analyzing your boss' personality may be an absolute necessity for anybody who works for a small-business owner.

You may believe that any businessperson will value you if you are a hustler filled with practical ideas for building business volume, size, and diversity. Not true, explains an expert who has wide university, consulting, and government-advisory experience with small businesses. People who were "pushed into" business by unemployment or fear of unemployment or retirement usually will resist your ideas. They simply want to chug along "making a living." Not only will they turn away from your expansion suggestions, but they may even regard you as a nuisance.

If you are bursting with ambition and inventive commercial plans, you need a small-business boss whose basic aim is making a lot of money or building an industrial empire. A boss like this will treasure you! However, in case you, too, just want to chug along, settle in with the first kind of small-business boss discussed above. And you will treasure each other!

## Supervisors Who Create Crises

At the end of the workday do you often say to yourself, "I've got to get out of this business; I can't take the pressure"? Maybe it's not the type of job you have that is creating strain; it may be the type of supervisor you work for.

Some supervisors function best under pressure. Consciously or subconsciously they create crises for themselves and for their workers. Supervisors with this kind of personality probably don't even realize what they are doing. Yet once you understand the pattern, bosses of this kind aren't hard to recognize. They are people who are very proud of their reputations for being able to manage "when the heat's on." They also make a point of insisting that "in business you've got to be able to take it." Even if they themselves complain about the frequent emergencies, they also clearly derive an emotional boost out of fighting through and coming out on top again.

Crisis-happy supervisors repeatedly manufacture situations by overreacting. They rush into action without taking time to really study the problem. For example, "We've all got to get that delivery made [or machine fixed or job completed or whatever] by quitting time tonight," they order. And everyone under them is forced to get up and run.

Yet if they'd stopped to think it through, they might have realized that sure, the problem is urgent. But a deadline of tomorrow night or two days from now would take care of it. Besides setting unrealistic deadlines, the crisis-plagued boss is often short of ability to foresee problems and to plan ahead.

If you recognize your own boss in this description, realize that it's not your occupation that's wearing you out. It's your boss. The same kind of work elsewhere with a noncrisis-creating supervisor might be very congenial.

### What Is Your Boss Afraid Of?

Under some circumstances, fear is a healthy and sensible reaction. But if you have trouble making sense of your boss' behavior, you may be working for someone who lives in a permanent state of fright and who has developed a bewildering personality as a result. A report in the *Advanced Management Journal* offered the theories of famed psychiatrist Karen Horney to explain bosses who are permanently terrified of being recognized as less of a person than they've tried to make themselves appear. "In some cases bosses are even afraid to let *themselves* know they're only human and that they . . . make mistakes as others do."

Bosses who suffer from this fear of making mistakes may show their anxiety by choosing one way to respond to all situations and sticking to that response regardless of whether or not it suits the situation.

Some bosses always act warm and friendly whether or not circumstances warrant such behavior. They never fire or demote incompetent employees. They bear with them or try to have them transferred. Nothing is important enough for them to argue or express strong feelings about. You should realize, however, that people like this are often tricky politicians underneath. Though they act unfailingly pleasant and absolutely refuse to confront any situation openly, they secretly try to get their way.

Other fearful bosses are always cold and distant. In good times they do the job assigned them, never adding anything new or different. They push papers around, fill out reports, make sure people come to work on time. When the pressure is on, these kinds of supervisors can be dangerous. They blame failure on everyone but themselves. And they spend considerable time collecting and presenting "facts" which "prove" that everybody *else* is guilty of incompetence.

A fearful boss cannot be cured. But you can protect yourself by never taking bosses like this at face value. You remain constantly aware that they are probably following the secretive behavior patterns we've outlined above. You keep records of projects you're given, date due, what you accomplished. You get them to put all important orders and changes in procedure in writing. If they dawdle, you write it down and send them a memo spelling out the facts as they were told you—and ask that they let you know immediately if you have misinterpreted anything. If you receive no answer, you're safe. Now keep a copy of your memo. In a showdown, a fearful boss will back off and avoid attacking someone who has records.

For day-to-day living you cling to the old axiom about actions speaking louder than words. You watch how these bosses' actions, body language, decisions, use of their time, etc., contradict their words. Then you believe that the actions represent the bosses' true goals and feelings.

## Why You May Not Get the Praise You Deserve

"My boss never compliments me, no matter how well I do my work" is one of the most common employee complaints.

Some bosses believe that paying a salary signifies sufficient approval, but they're bucking human nature. Industrial psychologists have repeatedly proved that people also need recognition and praise. Bosses who ignore this fact cheat themselves of the extra effort and loyalty their kind words would produce. However, the way you react to praise may well affect the amount of it you receive. Are you the type of person who, when you receive a compliment, relaxes and feels you can coast for a while? Your boss may have noticed that praise has this effect on you and may react accordingly. Or, when you're complimented, do you boast to everyone about it? Your supervisor may not like the impression you're creating of being a "favorite."

Finally, perhaps your expectations of praise are unreasonable. Do you wait for a rave every time you satisfactorily complete a task? You can't expect your boss to be bowled over daily by the fact that you're able to do your job; that's why you have it!

If you never seem to receive your fair share of recognition from a boss who does give deserved praise, one of your co-workers may be stealing credit for your accomplishments. If so, see that your supervisor finds out who contributed what.

# Boss Troubles, and What to Do About Them  6

In the preceding section we discussed learning to read your boss' mind and then turning what you discover to your own job advantage. In this section we're dealing with some important, specific boss-problems. We'll examine what causes them and how to cope.

We'll start with that prime requirement of successful job-manship: holding on to your job. Even when business is slow, some people remain employed. They are the ones who are either truly indispensable to the company or who have learned how to look indispensable. You'll find many practical ideas here that you can use to make sure that the boss realizes you are one of the must-stay people.

Other tough, real problems: When the chemistry is wrong between you and a co-worker, yet your supervisor wants you to work together on a project, how do you handle it? What of those dismal occasions when you realize that you and your supervisor are on opposing sides on some company issue? Is there anything you can do besides worry?

And lots more—including why you should hope your *boss* gets a big raise.

**How to Keep a Job When the Going Is Tough**

You are not alone if you sometimes worry about keeping your job. A certain amount of low-level job anxiety is probably normal for most people.

"Is my boss *really* satisfied with my work?" "Is anything going on in the company that might threaten my position?" These are thoughts that flit through people's minds even in good times.

For advice on how to help you strengthen your hold on your job, we created a panel of three experts who specialize in "boss psychology." We asked our panel, "How can people understand, relate to, and 'psyche out' their bosses with an eye to protecting their jobs?" Then we listed situations that you've probably faced and asked our panelists to provide us with practical guidelines and ideas that readers could put to use to "strengthen their hold on their jobs." Here are some of the questions we asked:

1. How can you protect your job when you have a new boss? How can you get the new boss to realize you're a good, competent worker? How do you avoid rubbing the new boss the wrong way during the settling-in period?
2. What can people do to make themselves and their job look "necessary" when business is bad for the company and job cutbacks are contemplated?
3. Even when things appear to be all right, how do you maintain and strengthen your position in your boss' eyes?

Our first panelist, psychologist Dr. Ernest Dichter of Dichter Associates International Ltd., is known as the "father of motivational research." During thirty-seven years as president of the Institute for Motivational Research and now as chairman of his present firm, Dr. Dichter has gained worldwide recognition as a master of understanding what makes people (including bosses) react as they do. He has solved problems of human behavior and motivations for many international companies, political organizations, and American and foreign governments. Obviously, when he gives advice about human behavior, he knows what he's talking about.

Dr. Dichter told us: To feel confident, relaxed, self-assured, and free of unnecessary anxiety in your relationship with your boss, there are *two* keys. If you use them, there won't be any need to worry about who is going to take your job. Dr. Dichter says:

> Psychologically, it is well known that *tactful* flattery, which is never refused by anyone, is best transmitted by imitation. What are some of the special ways that your boss organizes his/her office or desk? What is his/her approach when tackling a problem? Have you ever really paid attention? Does your boss have some special phrases, approaches, business methods?
>
> If you know how to reflect an almost duplicate image of some unique aspects of your boss' way of doing things, you've got a good start toward presenting yourself in a way that will get your boss to like you and your work. The psychological explanation is simple. The strength of self-love is well known. When bosses see

some unique aspects of themselves reflected in your behavior, it has to lead to acceptance of you. Otherwise, they would be rejecting themselves, which is contrary to normal human nature.

This is how it works. Assume you're a salesperson who sells a service or product that requires new customer contact on a regular basis. Tomorrow your supervisor will be travelling with you. What are some of the approaches, phrases, and key selling points that she/he uses about your product? If you use your supervisor's key selling points, key phrases, and you get the order, your boss has to feel good about you because you're using her/his approach. If you use her/his approach and don't land the order, what would the result be? "Ah, it was a lousy prospect, a bad customer—but your technique was great!" So even without getting the sale, you've maintained your position in your supervisor's eyes. But if you start using your own style and you fail, there you are the object of criticism.

The second necessity for establishing yourself firmly in your job is learning how to get feedback from your boss. Only through feedback can you keep track of what your boss is thinking. Then you can constantly adjust your performance. Without feedback you're only guessing.

Again, let's take the salesperson who's just completed a call, whether it's a sale or not. Instead of waiting anxiously for some direct comments, get your feedback by coming right out and saying, "O.K., how did I do; what do you think?" Even if you get the order, say, "I'm glad we got it. But what part of the visit do you think I ought to look at more closely?" Selling may not be your occupation. But whatever your work, by actively asking for feedback from your superior, you're getting the picture of what your boss wants you to do. At the same time you're demonstrating your desire to constantly improve, which is also bound to please.

Dr. Dichter emphasized that asking for feedback is useless unless you listen correctly. Many people, he explained, have preconceived notions of what their boss will say in a particular instance. When the comments do come, they've already tuned out. It's important, he said, to listen, not only to the words themselves, but to the emotion and attitudes that seem to be behind the words. "Are you listening to the tune of what your superior's hands are doing; are you watching body language? Have you bothered to read any books about body language? They're not only fun but they can really give you many insights into what people are really thinking when they're talking to you."

When you have a new boss, here are other ideas set forth by Dr. Dichter for protecting your job. If, as suggested previously, you are going to adapt yourself to the new boss' style, you should do some research. If he or she comes from within your company, do you know anyone he or she has worked with? Through these people, find out the new boss' work style, weaknesses, strengths, predilections. Even if the supervisor is from another company, effort on your part may turn up valuable information from someone in your company who interviewed her or him, someone who saw the new boss' résumé, someone who knows the new boss from a previous job. Dichter asks, "If it means strengthening your hold on your job or even keeping it, isn't this research worthwhile?"

Two of Ernest Dichter's other suggestions can reinforce your grip on your job by establishing you on good terms with any boss. The average person frequently complains about lack of recognition and lack of compliments from the boss. "Has it ever occurred to you," Dichter asks, "that your boss, too, has similar needs?" How long is it since you sincerely complimented your supervisor on something? Dichter continued:

> And when your job is threatened by business problems, you may make yourself more visible and your job look necessary by remembering that what most bosses want most is to be relieved of annoying details. Offering to take over some of your boss' small hassles or offering to come in on a Saturday morning or to stay late to reorganize the filing system or develop other time- and money-saving ideas would probably be viewed by your employer as real job motivation. This could help your boss see you as one of the people who are "essential" even during job cutback times.

Charles C. Vance, a Chicago-based member of our panel, is the author of *Boss Psychology* (McGraw-Hill), a guide to succeeding at your job by understanding your boss. The practical ideas he developed especially for us are based on his two decades of top-level human relations activities as an executive and as a consultant to more than sixty corporations, associations, and celebrities. Says Mr. Vance, "There are some suicidal things to avoid when a new boss or new owners arrive on the scene."

1. Don't tell the boss you had been hoping to get the job and you're disappointed that it went to her or him.
2. Don't start stabbing your old boss or old owner in the back.
3. Don't give the new people an earful of rumors and gossip about other members of your group.
4. Don't stay disinterestedly away from the new people, waiting for them to make the first overture toward friendliness.

Actions such as these, says Mr. Vance, quickly set you up in your superior's mind as a troublemaker. You may be shunted to one side or you may have created a situation where you'll soon be on your way out. But there are *positive* things that you should be doing.

Says he, "Things can get off to an incredibly bad start with a new supervisor at the outset," unless you do the following:

1. Hand the new boss *your job description.* How can bosses judge if you're competent or if they want to change your duties if they don't know what you're supposed to be doing?
2. Give the boss an "update." This report says, in effect, here are the assignments I was given in the last six months. Here's where I'm at on all of them.
3. Prepare a *brief* biography of yourself. Tell how long you've been with the company, what jobs you've held, what responsibilities you have, previous work experience, education, associations or business groups you belong to. Make it brief, but include all the *selling* points that will show the boss that you're active, involved, and competent.
4. Help the boss "learn the ropes" by saying, "If I can be of any help in showing you where things are or procedures that have been followed, please let me know." But give the boss time. Avoid pushing yourself into a supervisor's territory. When the boss does ask for help, be brief, concise, and businesslike.

"Remember, you are a question mark to the new boss. You must sell yourself and your capability. But it's the old story: sell, but not too hard or too fast. Trying to be an 'instant buddy' to your new supervisor can backfire!

"All businesses have sweet and sour times. When your particular area is facing the shattering job crunch, pay attention to the storm warnings. Management always hastens to allow you to share fully in the fear and anxiety of distressing business times. Budget cutbacks, immediate layoffs of what management calls 'dead wood,' notices of belt-tightening on the bulletin boards, doleful stories in the house newspaper—all serve to make a nervous wreck of you. You can protect your interests under these 'hanging noose' conditions by following these safety guidelines:

1. Remember that a jittery management wants *visual reassurance* that its people are indeed working hard. Report to work early. Stay at your desk or work station instead of visiting around. Be busy all day. If you don't have enough work, make some. If you feel it can be done within the framework of your job, ask your boss for more assignments. Cut out the coffee breaks or take coffee to your spot and consume it while you work. Put in some overtime. A half-hour every other evening will help. Take work home once or twice a week—and let your boss know it. Take a shorter lunchtime. Brown-bag it at your desk as often as you can. Keep that 'visual reassurance' always in mind and make yourself highly visible to your boss.

2. Don't take chances that your superior knows exactly how much you're contributing and doing. Report progress as often as you can without being a nuisance. Give the boss written reports on your assignments. If you can swing it, sit with the boss to go over it. You are important to your boss in direct relationship with the degree that the boss understands how well you are doing your job, that you are dependable, and that you are contributing ideas for cutting costs and improving profits. The name of the game for all business still is to make a profit. Show your boss you are 'profit conscious.'"

Our third expert, Eli Djeddah, is an outstandingly successful employment counsellor who has headed the New York, Boston, and San Francisco offices of Bernard Haldane Associates for twelve years and is now president of Eli Djeddah Associates,

Executive Development Services, in San Diego. During these years, he has worked with and helped place five thousand men and women. In order to succeed and guide and place his clients, he has had to develop clear insight into what a boss wants. He is the author of *Moving Up* (Lippincott), a lively book of advice on how to find and land the job you've always wanted, and of *Which Side Is Up?* (Ten Speed Press), which discusses the human behavior elements of successful living.

Mr. Djeddah's first point is so simple, yet so fundamental, that many of us may overlook it: "The best way to get any boss, new or old, to realize that you are a good, competent worker is simply to be one. Beyond that, be truthful with yourself. If you hate your job, can't stand the people you work with, and don't want to tackle the problems the job produces, why should a boss value you? And why should you struggle to stay?

"With a new boss, don't persist in fighting changes required by the new supervisor. Keep in mind that the new boss is feeling pressured and anxious by new responsibilities. These anxieties often cause a new supervisor to be highly sensitive to criticism almost to the point of paranoia. Ears and eyes of a new boss can often record even your most subtle indication of disapproval. So accept your new boss' ways or leave. Don't criticize, not even when you're alone in your sleep."

Other of Djeddah's ideas are equally incisive. Says he: "With either a new or an established boss, when a problem arises that should be brought to your supervisor's attention, never bring up the problem unless you have a suggested solution or solutions! Dumping problems on bosses without solutions makes them wonder what use you are to them. Instead, go to your boss and say, 'A problem has developed that I think you'd want to be informed about. Here are the possible solutions which I've evaluated according to their strengths and weaknesses. Could I have your advice?' When you let the boss choose, you've accomplished your end. By producing the solutions, you've demonstrated your value, even if the boss finally decides on a totally different resolution. Now if the chosen remedy goes wrong, your boss must share the responsibility. If it goes right, you've done your job well. Unless you've been completely stupid with your suggestions, your

boss will like you because you have allowed his superior judg-
ment to save the day. Equally important, whenever you go to
bosses with solutions for them to choose from, you are being
educated in their priorities—which is another way of saying
you're being educated in the things you should be doing to
succeed."

Djeddah explains that understanding the real power lines of
your place of employment is essential in both good business times
and bad. All the people with titles *don't* have all the authority.
Sometimes a person who carries no title at all can have more
power and influence on your job future than a vice-president.
This is a long process of listening and observing actions and
reactions.

Djeddah cautions against pushing for egocentric gains when
business is bad. Don't ask for a salary increase, an extended vacation, a new car, more help to do your job, or even for a new desk
blotter, unless it is absolutely essential. This is the time to make
yourself visible as someone who is working for the good of the
company, not simply for yourself.

His years of experience have convinced Djeddah that the
quickest and most reliable way to find out the style and values
of new bosses or new owners is to talk to them. He says, "There
is a Mideast folk saying, 'He who is shy with his wife gets no
children.' How can you support your owners' or bosses' battles
if you don't talk to them and find out what they're battling for?"

And strive always to make yourself into a pleasant co-worker.
It is a fact of business life that people lose their jobs more quickly
because of personality conflicts than because of incompetence.
Djeddah phrases it positively as, "Acceptance is more important
than competence," adding, "Any enemy you make is always too
powerful, even if at the moment the enemy seems to be a completely unimportant person, a pigmy with a toothpick. But every
ally you can develop will eventually be an aid to you in your
efforts to keep a firm hold on your job."

Dr. Dichter summed up our experts' advice: "If you're not
willing to make the extra effort to really understand your boss
and and then follow through in your own job interest, perhaps
you ought to reevaluate what you're doing in your current
position."

## Three Other Ways to Escape a Company Layoff

Are people in other departments disappearing? Don't just assume they've quit! Find out.

Is your boss stiff and self-conscious with you? Most bosses hate to fire, and their guilt feelings when they are readying themselves for the "termination interview" may make them behave unnaturally when you're together.

In his book, *Jobkeeping*, David Noer suggests some ways to save your job when you see a layoff looming:

1. Be cautious about accepting departmental transfers or even promotions. Many companies lay off by seniority. In a new department or new echelon, you'll be last in and probably the first out. However, accepting a transfer to a different geographical location may be clever. After spending all that money moving you, the company may be reluctant to dismiss you.

2. Ride out the layoff period by asking for a leave of absence. Employers are obliged to make every effort to provide re-employment after a military absence, so if you have Reserve or National Guard obligations, what better time to volunteer for active duty!

3. Save and use the good news. "When layoffs are in the air," says Noer, "anyone can employ this technique, including the salesperson with a major order in his pocket, the accountant with a new tax angle, the office worker with a new procedure to increase productivity." Withhold the news till your job appears threatened, then produce it, making sure to impress

upon your superior that, in order to make full use of this new development, you must be kept on the scene.

**Danger Signals: Are You Heading for a Firing?**

Are you in danger of being fired? Of course, nobody knows for certain except your boss. But some of the following are often danger signs of supervisor-employee friction or dissatisfaction which may prompt your boss to think about replacing you or pressuring you into quitting.

1. Do your supervisor's reactions and style of working rub you the wrong way? Chances are, if his or her personality grates on you, he or she is a very different kind of person from you. Therefore, your way of doing things is probably irritating your boss!

2. It may not only be your work style but your private life that differs significantly from the boss'. If you, your family, your social life, your athletic skill, your education, or anything else about you is clearly better than what your supervisor is getting out of life, you may be making him/her feel inferior. Or if your politics, religious commitment, or even your personal style with the opposite sex are opposed to his outlook, you may be making him feel hostile. And nobody, certainly not your boss, is going to be pleased with those two feelings.

3. Within the company itself, keep alert for turnover when there's a new supervisory team with new ideas, or when there's a distinct change in company policy. And always stay agile if you find yourself supervised by someone who hasn't a kind

word to say for any of the former employees. If none of them could please—well, what more can we say?

## The False-Front Boss

You've noticed at work that problems wait, problems multiply, and new problems develop. Though there's plenty of "action" coming from your boss, few things ever seem really to get settled. Why? You may have a boss who is fearful of making decisions. Bosses like this may survive for a long time through behavior which gives the impression they're doing something when they're not.

Henry O. Golightly, president of the consulting firm Golightly & Company International, has analyzed the no-decision bosses. Common tactics of such a boss are: (A) He considers your ideas and turns them down with a consistent "The timing just isn't right" (certainly this can be a realistic comment but, used too often, it can be a tip-off to an executive who's avoiding decisions); (B) Appoints a committee to "study" or "investigate" whenever anything has to be decided; (C) Creates a smoke screen. For example, faced with having to decide about buying some expensive equipment, a no-decision boss may create a smoke screen by insisting that what's really needed are workers of greater experience and skill. Maybe these people aren't obtainable. Yet this smoke screen issue distracts others and diffuses the pressure to make a decision about the equipment. And lastly, when a difficult decision seems unavoidable, decision-shy supervisors will find an excuse to take a trip. They'll look over sales opportunities, attend a business convention, make a speech—anything to get away—meanwhile hoping the matter will somehow be settled in their absence.

If you feel you have a good idea and are suffering with a no-decision boss, you may be able to help yourself by taking advantage of another characteristic of such supervisors: their great desire to pass the buck. You may be able to obtain power to carry out your idea by encouraging this kind of superior to pass the authority to you. Accepting the responsibility and making the decision yourself may be the only way you'll ever get issues decided.

## A Warning to Bosses' Pets

You may have the boss' go-ahead for extra days off, a variable lunch hour, or other privileges, but you're going to create jealous fury among your co-workers if you don't handle your privileges properly.

Unless they're absolutely essential, extra privileges can be booby traps. Your co-workers are quite logically going to resent you and your easier life! When a personal crisis *does* require special work concessions, it's important for everyone to understand the reason. For example, one woman whose child had leukemia explained matters to her boss. But, unwilling to be an object of pity, she mentioned nothing to her co-workers. The entire office staff was soon livid with resentment at her erratic attendance record and the boss' apparent willingness to "let her get away with it."

## When You're in Conflict
## with Your Boss

If you want to stay with your job, forget about battling it out. You can't win. The boss has the power. Says business consultant Charles C. Vance, "When you realize the boss is angry with you, go to him/her and say, 'I'm puzzled by what happened. Will you explain it to me?' *Then listen.* Control any of your emotions that stupidly urge you to get angry or protest. When the boss finishes say, 'I see the situation more clearly now. Here is what I think can be done to clear it up.'" This returns life to normal between the two of you. At the same time, it marks you as a sensible, responsible person to have in the organization.

Never allow yourself to begin the encounter with a preconceived idea of what your boss is going to say. For example, if you're late with some project, do you think you already know what the spiel will be and have you already tuned out? When possible, take notes as the boss talks. Under the emotional stress of the moment, your memory can play tricks on you. With notes, you're not open to the danger of later overlooking what the boss considers the most important point of the entire discussion.

## How Your Boss' Pay Affects Yours

Mighty few people lie awake nights worrying about the size of their boss' paycheck. Maybe that ought to change. If you're a good worker, your chances for fair pay may be tied to how fairly the boss thinks he/she is being paid.

At Carnegie-Mellon University, managers, project engineers, and others involved in salary decisions took part in an experiment. They were divided into four groups. Group 1 was told, "Pretend you're a high-performing, good boss being well paid." Groups 2, 3, and 4 were told, respectively, to pretend: "You're a high-performing, good boss but you're not being paid what you're worth"; "You're doing a poor job as a boss but you're being well paid"; "You're doing a poor job as a boss and you're being poorly paid."

Then the four groups were given an imaginary $2,400 to divide up among their imaginary subordinates, some of whom were described as good workers and some as poor workers. *All the results pointed to bosses adjusting their subordinates' pay to match the way their own was being treated.* Good bosses receiving good pay (Group 1) showed a strong tendency to reward good workers under them with good pay and to penalize poor workers with poor pay. The lucky supervisors in Group 3 who were performing badly but being highly paid were the most generous. Apparently aware of their good luck, they handed out the maximum amount possible. But, mirroring their own situation, there was little difference in raises they awarded competent workers as compared to those awarded incompetent workers.

Those who fared the worst worked under high-performing bosses who felt they weren't being paid adequately. "If the company is going to be tight with me, I'm going to be tight with subordinates," wrote one of these bosses. All of which may mean that if you want more money in your pay envelope, you ought to hope the bosses get more in theirs.

# If You're a Supervisor 7

Most of the business advice that pours from the American press deals with how to be a successful supervisor. Organizations such as the American Management Associations publish monthly magazines devoted entirely to the subject. Publishers annually send forth thousands of pamphlets, leaflets, trade newsletters, and books, all directed at the "manager's needs." Self-employed business consultants and hired minions of giant consulting firms jet about the United States covering millions of air miles each year, as they are called east, west, north, and south to advise management on how to raise the level of their supervisory performance.

These same consulting organizations, together with colleges and private specialists of all kinds, annually schedule scores of one-to-five-day seminars on supervisory techniques. Managers from all over the United States regularly gather in the ballrooms of motels and hotels of large cities to "share, listen, and learn." Fees of $300–$500 per participant for two or three days are regarded as "reasonable" and are typical.

So many people make a good living giving advice to supervisors because supervising isn't easy. There really aren't any short, pat answers. If there were, there wouldn't be so many intelligent people flailing about trying to find them.

The basic problem lies in the fact that slavery is illegal. You can't whip a person into doing what you want. Nor can you terrify people into docile job obedience: jobs are relatively plentiful, and unemployment insurance and welfare provide an economic floor. A supervisor can still give orders and expect to see some results. But to achieve really excellent results, a supervisor has to learn to win workers' cooperation, to motivate them to perform even when the supervisor isn't watching. It can be done. But it's an art that is the result partly of instinct and partly of methodically learning how to do it. This section deals with some of the how-to's.

In it we offer many insights valuable to the supervisor that can be obtained *nowhere else*. The long subsection on "The Ten Leading Gripes About Bosses" is the result of a nationwide poll in more than three hundred newspapers conducted especially for this report. Most published business advice that discusses "what workers want from supervisors" is based on academic intellectualizing, limited psychological experiments, or the personal experience of the individual writer. This report is based on the reactions of an enormous cross-section of workers in all of the states of the Union except Hawaii.

Similarly, at a time when competent secretarial help is in chronically short supply and becoming even scarcer, we bypassed the flood of advice by self-appointed experts on what secretaries want. Instead we went to the secretaries themselves. Through *P.S. for Private Secretaries*, which has been inviting and discussing secretaries' complaints for almost two decades, we were able to reach to the core of what a supervisor has to do to keep a competent secretary happy.

The rest of this section offers other seldom-discussed basic facts which can help you remain or become a successful supervisor.

## The Ten Leading Gripes About Bosses

"Send Us Your Complaints About Your Boss!" we said in a "Jobmanship" column in *Family Weekly*. "Tell us what your boss does that confuses you, makes it hard for you to do your job properly, or hurts your feelings. And what does he/she do that you think is unfair, unreasonable, or just plain stupid?"

Considering that "happily married" couples sometimes argue and parents and children squabble, it's not surprising that strangers may develop friction points when they work as bosses and subordinates. And just as there are often two sides to a family dispute, so in a business family gripe between boss and subordinate there well may be more than one side to the story.

From the employees' viewpoint, our letters made it clear that there are ten common boss errors. The boss-gripes airmailed to *Family Weekly* from Alaskan and West Coast readers matched those which piled in from the Midwest, South, and East.

Many gripes had a wistful air. The feeling they projected was, "My boss is really nice. If he/she knew this gripe bothered me, I think my boss might try to do something about it. I wish I knew how to tell him/her." Perhaps this article will do the job. Supervisors reading the gripes may quietly recognize a situation in their organizations. At the same time they may feel, "I'd sure like to tell the people who work for me my side of this."

Other gripes were from people who felt their superiors were unreasonable. "Just print this problem and a group of us will tack it on the bulletin board" and "Please print this and I'll send it underlined to the boss" were frequent pleas in our letters. It's easy to understand that bluntly telling the boss "the truth" in this fashion can seem like a quick solution. But it's not recommended unless you're *sure* your boss is definitely wrong and that he/she has the kind of personality that will alter behavior when slammed with naked criticism.

One revelation shone through all the letters. Apparently success as a boss doesn't depend on a formal education, the kind of work you do, or even the general goodness of your character. "I have a fine, dedicated boss (he's a doctor)," one of our correspondents wrote. "His first interest is the welfare of his patients and we admire him for it. However, when one of us makes a mistake, even a minor one like a handprint on the wall, he launches into a tirade in front of other employees and patients. . . . It can last fifteen minutes or even forty-five minutes and the offenders are usually reduced to tears!" Or as a factory worker put it, "My gripes include foremen who were good skilled craftsmen but who aren't leaders."

A secretary at a community college did a good job of summing up the overall problem as many employees see it: "Too many people are elevated to administrative levels without administrative training." Our survey seemed to confirm her outlook. We found that school principals, doctors, dentists, social workers, labor leaders, nursing supervisors, and other highly educated professionals were indicted by their subordinates almost as often as were business people, foremen, shop owners, and office supervisors.

Not *all* school principals, doctors, foremen, shop owners, etc., of course. By asking for gripes we inevitably drew our answers from those who feel they have problem bosses. Tension, emotion, and raw nerve endings crackled through our mail. Some correspondents acknowledged that the top person's behavior might result from pressures on him or her. Overall, though, readers responding to our invitation for boss-complaints sketched a picture of many supervisors who seem ill-equipped to work with people.

Probably the most extreme description of the turmoil that poor boss-subordinate relations can cause came from a fireman. "My boss is a fire chief and there are eighty people who consider him their boss. He is malicious . . . a liar . . . has a terrible temper. If you disagree with him or even try to give an opinion that differs from his, he completely blows his cool. He never compliments—all he ever does is find fault. It is so bad that some fire captains under him honestly try to do what they think the fire chief wants done instead of paying attention to the fire or the emergency."

To all this the fire chief might retort, "I have to combine the actions of all the fire company into an effective team. In the middle of a fire I haven't time to justify every order." But even if his fire-fighting tactics are exemplary, this chief hasn't succeeded in creating a satisfactory rapport with his crew. Consequently, everyone suffers because the firemen seethe with a very negative attitude toward him as a boss.

Based on our survey, what we offer are insights into how people view their problems with their bosses in their own minds. The prestigious American Management Associations has discussed the question at various of its national management seminars. "Real or imaginary," says one of the AMA's program chairmen, "a serious complaint has to be considered. As long as the person *thinks a problem exists, his behavior will reflect that problem and it therefore does exist."*

First and far in the lead in our survey as the Number One boss-gripe:

1. *"The boss treats us employees like 'things.' Makes us feel frustrated, small, humiliated, and stupid. Displays no knowledge of human relations."*

This is a puzzling situation. From the 1920s, when psychology was first popularized, till today, with its emphasis on personality and self-expression, we Americans have been deluged with newspaper, magazine, book, and TV advice about everyone's basic need to be appreciated as an individual. In addition, business publications have endlessly discussed psychologists Maslow's and Hertzberg's conclusions that all people work, not only for money, but for recognition, appreciation, and a sense of achievement.

Some wounded feelings are probably inflicted unintentionally. For instance, bosses may sometimes forget to say "good morning," not because they intend to slight their subordinates, but because they are preoccupied with problems. However, our mail indicates that masses of people, though allowing for the human factor, wish supervisors would check their good image of themselves against their real, everyday actions. Pressure to get work out or insensitivity, subordinates report, often causes managers to under-utilize any human-relations knowledge they may have.

Over and over again, we heard the complaint, "The boss considers subordinates to be objects—much the same as typewriters or copying machines. He uses us, his 'objects,' to further his own ends." Or, from a restaurant worker, "Sometimes he really makes me feel about an inch high." Or, "I am a nurse, but my supervisor makes me feel like a robot." Another said, "Each of my three bosses treats his subordinates like dogs, with a sadistic contempt for their capabilities. You just don't treat human beings that way." A bank official vividly described his problem: "Though I know my business well, the manager constantly interrupts when we're explaining things to customers. Sometimes it's like a tennis match with the customer looking back and forth. This makes us look like dummies."

Nor are physical strength and a tough job reasons to ignore human needs. "I'm a construction worker. The company is run by two brothers who are self-made men. Unfortunately neither has the slightest idea of good employee relations." And the top prize for how to humiliate someone through human-relations carelessness goes for this: "I really like my boss. But there are two secretaries in our office, and when introductions are made, my boss always says about the other girl, 'Meet my *beautiful* secretary.' Then he turns to me and says, 'And this is my other secretary.' I realize I haven't been endowed with great beauty, but—"

Why should bosses bother listening to the first complaint and to the other nine complaints our survey discovered? Because by doing so, they may be able to head off trouble for themselves. Industrial psychologists long ago discovered that workers who feel humiliated and frustrated, consciously or subconsciously develop all manner of subtle ways to get back at their supervisors by lowering production and compounding on-the-job problems. Furthermore, our letters disclosed that managers who fail to act in response to widespread, reasonable complaints are eventually faced with a predicament where "the turnover around here is terrific, yet the ones in charge haven't a clue to the real reasons."

2. *"If he only knew it, we'd do anything for a compliment, for a pat on the head (or the back) occasionally. . . . The payoff is not just in the paycheck."*

It's impossible to discuss the yearning for kind words in phrases better than those our correspondents used. "Not one word of credit does he give to the help that put him where he is." "He will not comment on the 99 percent of a project that was accomplished well; only on the 1 percent that wasn't up to his standards." "My boss will agree with someone else who mentions that I'm efficient, but he won't ever tell me!" "I realize workers should always strive to do a good job; after all, that's what they're being paid for. But a boss could just throw out a few encouraging words once in a while."

Even simple "Thank you" comments are rationed by thoughtless supervisors. "I've done extra work, such as fixing new tax lists when taxes changed, doing this at home at night. I never even get thanked for it." "Once in a while my boss could say, 'Thank you.' I never hear those words."

3. *"My boss isn't fair! The boss has favorites who get the promotions, pay increases, special privileges."*

This is a complaint that's tricky to interpret. While some bosses are certainly guilty of uneven behavior toward different people, especially where family is involved ("We need a good hot article on nepotism," declared one outraged letter writer), some "favoritism" may be in the eye of the beholder. Before working yourself into a fury about the boss' pets, ask yourself if the "favorite" really is more reliable and efficient than you. What is your attitude toward your work, your boss, your company? If *you* were the boss, would you prefer yourself or others as employees?

At the same time, there's no doubt that personality factors play an ever-increasing role in job success. In today's world, sociologists and industrial psychologists have discovered that skill in getting along with co-workers may be as important or even more important than work output in determining promotions and general progress. Still, stark cases of favoritism, such as "The boss let him have an extra week's vacation when he turned us all down. . . . There's revolution brewing here," prove how essential it is for a supervisor to carefully monitor himself/herself.

4. *"My boss is very disorganized."*

Many letters softened this criticism by starting, "My boss is nice but—" "We never know what to do. He says one thing one day, contradicts himself the next." "My boss puts things off. Then on Fridays it's rush, rush, rush. This is hard to swallow sometimes, especially when work's been somewhat slow till Friday."

No one explanation can cover every disorganized boss. Sometimes the top person's strength is in creative ability, technical knowledge, or sales, and not in organization management. Other times, bosses may be avoiding aspects of their jobs which they dislike or find tedious or difficult. And, very frequently, what appears to be disorganization or contradiction is, in fact, the inevitable effect of those daily changes in the work world which pressure the manager to alter priorities, methods, and deadlines if objectives are to be reached.

5. *"Rewards for good work and attendance aren't visible."*

Constantly, this same deep disappointment was voiced. "I've worked for the medical center for two years, making all the salads for 168 patients, plus sometimes the cafeteria, and have had to beg for every raise I got. I now earn 10¢ above the new bare legal minimum. Sometimes it gets frustrating racing the clock. I figure if I'm doing two people's jobs, I should get paid more. . . . I was going to quit and my boss said I'd get a raise and new position. Well, I didn't, and now they've put a new girl over me as assistant supervisor. I have been there in snow and other hard times when they couldn't depend on anyone else. I am never late and I can do any job there, including cook. It seems like I have worked hard for nothing and they sure don't appreciate it."

"I had no idea that places like this mill still existed. I make less than the legal minimum wage an hour. People who have been here about thirty years make about the legal minimum and get no sick or retirement pay." Or, "My boss doesn't think clerical help have to work for a living. . . . He hires at rock-bottom salaries."

In a recent article in the influential business publication *Wharton Quarterly*, Dr. David Sirota points out that supervisors often deal with people in too simplistic a fashion, i.e., ascribing all worker behavior to a single goal. Dr. Sirota explains that if many managers overlook emotional needs (as we discussed under No. 1), others have mistakenly decided that a compliment, "recognition," and good human relations are *all* they need offer. Our letters prove that the manager who relies too strongly on job enrichment and human relations while stinting on raises and wages is laying up the deepest kind of anti-boss hostility against himself.

6. *"My boss' personal habits are mean, outrageous, dishonest, or disgusting."*

"My boss is sneaky. He stands at the foot of the stairs and eavesdrops, and he listens to our phone conversations." "He smells as if his deodorant isn't working." "He is always snooping into my personal life and it is none of his business."

7. *"I'm so tired of being blamed unfairly for things others do."*

As people hunger for praise, so too are they willing to accept blame, if only the blame is merited and the reprimand is made tactfully. "And when he reprimands, it's never done behind closed doors but during business hours in front of a houseful of customers or wherever he finds you. Sometimes it's done over the loudspeaker, which makes it all the lovelier!"

8. *"The boss does not allow for employees having ideas or brains."*

This complaint reflects boss-employee relationships that are strained because the person in charge has a poor understanding of how to work with people. If complaints Nos. 1 and 6 expose problems in getting along with others on a human level, this one reveals insufficient knowledge of how to motivate subordinates to do a good job. One woman wrote, "He tells me each and every duty to perform even after five years, when nearly one hundred percent of the time I answer, 'It's already been done!' " And from a woman whose male boss is younger than she is, "Any sign of initiative seems to terrify him." And the comment from exasperated wage earners everywhere is "The boss always acts as if you're not doing anything no matter how much you produce."

And from all parts of the entire United States arises a chorus of "They will never admit they are wrong about anything" and "They always try to give the impression that because they're the boss they're somehow superior beings." (This gripe raises the question: If bosses did admit error, what treatment could they expect from their employees? Would they gossip, joke, and remind them of it ever after?)

9. *"The boss discriminates against older workers or against women."*

"A girl in our office who returned after a meager three-week maternity leave with no pay lost her seniority. But a man in the office who was off work for four weeks with back trouble didn't lose a bit of seniority and he drew full pay those four weeks." "No chance for promotion around here just because I'm a woman." And from older Americans, "Most jobs won't hire you, no matter how intelligent, experienced, and capable you are if you're in your fifties or sixties unless they need a low-paid sweeper or janitor." "At meetings the boss is always saying the older employees made all the mistakes. It's the exact opposite!"

The many people suffering from gripe No. 9 may be in both the best and worst positions of all boss-criticizers—the best position because laws and recent court decisions awarding hundreds of millions of dollars in equal-pay and equal-opportunity damages to women have created a business climate in which companies are at last being pressured into hiring and promoting women for significant jobs. Yet, older workers of both sexes may also be in the worst of positions because discrimination against senior citizens, though it too is illegal, is often harder to prove in court. Or is it? Is the weak record of older workers in battling job discrimination simply the result of their being less active than women in their own legal behalf?

10. *"My boss has a dirty mind and enjoys saying things that are ambiguous. But the sly glance he gives me relays the message of a dirty mind."*

And from another employee, "Oh, the language he uses on the phone when someone crosses him!"; or, "We all wish he'd keep the tales of his sex life out of business hours."

Though it's true that during the last decade some people have altered their standards of what constitutes appropriate language and subject matter in a business setting, not everyone has adopted the new ideas. A wise boss has to keep that fact in mind. Some supervisors apparently push crudely beyond even present-day limits.

Why do people stay on their jobs when their bosses have so numerous and so serious a list of failings? Those who can leave often do so. Others, trapped by age, a slack job market in their skill, or seniority rights they need to protect, sigh and hang on. Others feel their superior's virtues outweigh his faults. But many people who see themselves as trapped echoed the orthodontist's assistant's explanation: "I stay because I love the work I do. Yet I can hardly bear to go in each day." If love for the kind of work you do is the reason you stay with an incompatible boss, ask yourself if, in your locale, you couldn't do the same kind of job for someone else or for another company.

One other comment was laced regularly through the gripe-mail: "Thanks for the chance to sound off. Knowing I'm not alone and that others have gripes about bosses makes me feel better already."

## Fourteen Complaints Secretaries Have About Bosses—and Some Solutions

Sometimes when there's a problem, people forget to ask the real experts. For example, as demand for competent secretaries has risen during the last few years, everyone from personnel manager to corporation president has issued lists of do's and don'ts for creating goodwill between boss and secretary. But it's difficult to find any in-depth study of what secretaries themselves want and don't want in a job and in a boss.

Since 1960, *P.S. for Private Secretaries,* a twice-weekly newsletter of information for secretaries published by the Bureau of Business Practice, Inc., has featured a lively section called "Secretarial Clinic." From all over the United States and Canada, secretaries write to air their job problems and to request advice from other secretaries. We asked Mrs. Irene Stone, editor of *P.S. for Private Secretaries,* to review her files of letters and find the most important problems and complaints voiced by the secretaries.

As you read the list, remember no secretary may ever tell you any of these things directly, not even if she* quits. Long ago, industrial psychologists proved that most people don't tell the

*Though we use "she" for secretary, we do realize that approximately 5 percent of secretaries in the United States today are men.

complete truth when they leave. Typical explanations such as "I need a job closer to home," "My husband doesn't want me to work," and "My children's school lets out earlier than it used to" lull a boss into believing her departure wasn't prompted by a dislike of the job, and certainly not because of him. But an alert supervisor has to realize that in many cases a secretary would keep the job, regardless of inconveniences—if she enjoyed it sufficiently.

Many people do not understand that being a boss in the late twentieth century in a democratic society is a complicated skill. Far more is involved than just giving sensible orders. The first two kinds of secretarial complaints make this fact clear:

1. Their methods of dealing with people are difficult to understand and they have aroused a great deal of resentment.
2. They don't know much about office procedures and sharing ideas with others. They are inconsiderate and immature and won't readily accept new ideas or other people's ideas.

In our modern, classless society, the power of the boss' position can take a boss just so far. Tact and human-relations skill are business necessities. Says an expert quoted in *Personnel Journal:* "The difference between the people who have a top-notch secretary and those who do not, may be the men or women themselves. Personnel departments can do just so much for a boss in finding candidates . . . but the rest is up to the executive—the interviewing, training, and willingness to share responsibility with the new assistant."

Other important complaints indicate that some bosses may be so busy pushing through their day's output that they become insensitive to the fact that secretaries are *people.*

3. Bosses expect too much of one person.
4. They don't believe in vacations for secretaries. But they don't mind giving me extra duties or asking me to work overtime without extra pay. And they rarely express their appreciation.
5. I work for more than one person and get conflicting assignments.

When any of these situations occurs *regularly,* it tells a secretary her boss doesn't think enough of her to develop a reasonable overall work load for her; nor does he/she consider how many hours are needed for her to carry out individual tasks he/she assigns. The problem runs far deeper than inconvenience—though that in itself is serious. As one secretary put it, "When he acts like that, I feel like an extension of the office furniture. Sure, he's routinely polite, but I can't help feeling he values me as just a cog that's useful to him."

A recent job-turnover survey of office workers revealed that when a secretary believes her boss has stopped seeing her as a person, her mind often turns to job-hunting.

This complaint is an excellent example of chronic personality conflict between boss and secretary:

6. They are too stiff to work for. There's never any variation from the norm.

Problems like this are no one's *fault*. Yet in any job, personality differences can induce a feeling of chronic fatigue when endured five days a week, eight hours a day. Other personality-conflict examples:

7. My boss and I are both "drivers"—and sometimes our drives conflict.
8. We're both sticklers for detail, and sometimes our ideas of detail differ.

It all depends on how serious the personality conflict seems to the secretary involved. Suggesting that a person "adjust"—especially the secretary—is one usual solution. Frankly, though, for a competent secretary there are plenty of good jobs in the world. If problems like Nos. 6, 7, and 8 become really important to her, probably the healthiest solution is a change of position to a boss whose temperament is more congenial.

And then there's the famous go-fer, or personal-chores, problem:

9. My boss asks me to handle personal chores, like buying gifts for his wife, typing his son's term paper, etc.

Though *P.S. for Private Secretaries* found that this is one of the fourteen most common complaints secretaries make against their bosses, there is a wide range of secretarial reaction. Some secretaries were informed when they accepted the position that they'd be expected to do such chores. Others object, not to the work itself, but to how they're asked. They prefer, "Do you have time to . . . ?" or "Would you mind. . . ?" This provides the opportunity to refuse graciously. It also indicates the boss realizes that personal services *are* favors.

Still other secretaries say they don't mind personal chores "as long as I have my lunch hour and after-work hours free, and can do the personal typing, bookkeeping, and shopping on company time." And yet another group of secretaries is adamant in finding all these tasks demeaning!

If No. 9 is an old problem, No. 10 is rather new. More so than in the past, many secretaries today are ambitious for responsibility and promotion:

10. They are unwilling to turn loose some detail work that only clutters their desks and day.

In a "Be Nicer to Secretaries" memo issued by the State Department, the government admonished bosses who don't recognize a secretary's intelligence, expand her authority, and ultimately, if she wants it, offer her a promotion. "Do not assume secretaries to have disabling intellectual limitations" was the government's way of putting it.

The last four complaints may not seem very important to a busy supervisor. Yet year in and year out secretaries write emotion-charged appeals about these situations to the Secretarial Clinic. Nothing that produces so much emotion can be dismissed as trivial.

11. Bosses don't tell me the things I should know ahead of time.
12. They leave their offices without telling me where they are going around the building.
13. They neglect to tell me when they'll be out of town on a business trip, or just where they are when they are out of the building.
14. Sometimes both my bosses go out and forget to come back when I have an appointment for lunch.

As one desperate secretary put it in a letter to the Clinic: "The worst part is that my boss frequently disappears just as I receive a long-distance call for him or before someone from another department drops in to see him. How do I correct this, short of hanging a bell around his neck?"

Little things attended to, we've all often been told, create contentment. Problems No. 11–14 make it obvious that little things, regularly ignored, can roil emotions and even create deep resentment.

Overall, being aware of the other person's reactions is probably the best way for a boss and secretary to solve the fourteen commonest conflict situations.

## On-the-Job Compliments: What's the Real Story?

Do supervisors often express appreciation for a job well done? One cause of friction between supervisors and workers is revealed by the completely contrasting answers the two groups give to that question. Somebody is fooling himself or is not paying attention to what's *really* happening each day on the job. But who? Just look at the following results of a recent psychological investigation.

In the investigation almost 90 percent of the workers responded, "My supervisor doesn't often show appreciation for a good job. Neither do I get more responsibility, a pat on the back, or training for a better job. Good work doesn't even get me very much wholehearted praise."

But when the supervisors of these same people were asked how and when they reward good work, 80 percent replied, "I give a pat on the back and thorough praise very often." More than half of the supervisors believe that they "very often" reward good work with privileges, training for better jobs, and by giving more interesting assignments.

This same double vision appeared in another study. "How does a person get ahead in this company?" people were asked.

"Merit," said the supervisors. "Knowing the right people or luck," declared the workers.

Somebody's fooling himself, but who?

## How Supervisors Misunderstand What Workers Want

Supervisors often give completely wrong answers when asked what workers want. As a result of the supervisors' confusion, all kinds of needless supervisor-worker hassles can develop.

Industrial psychologists have zeroed in on supervisors' two most serious mistakes in understanding workers' goals: (A) believing that money and other material payments are the only incentives that interest workers and, (B) not understanding how very important on-the-job social contacts are to people.

Immediately after security items such as steady work and pensions, getting along with co-workers and supervisors is the major concern of job holders. And *office personnel* value their job contacts almost as highly. Yet when supervisors were asked about workers' priorities, their answers showed how off-base their beliefs really were. They were running their areas on the assumption that workers place very little or *no* importance on co-worker and supervisor contacts.

For example, one group of supervisors tried guessing how many people would keep working if they inherited a good income. Their guesses were wildly inaccurate. They guessed that about two-thirds of the workers would *not* want to work if they inherited wealth. The workers' reaction was they'd be bored without their job and job-social contacts. And 65 percent of factory and 69 percent of office personnel said, income or not, they would continue on the job.

For years hundreds of technical articles have explained workers' social and psychological wants. Yet the confusion remains. Perhaps a non-technical summary such as this may help provide a clearer understanding of workers' true priorities.

# Why Supervisors and Managers Don't Understand Each Other

If you're caught in a supervisor vs. manager tussle, this may help. First-line supervisors are the people who direct the work of first-rung employees. Managers are the people who direct a group of supervisors. These two groups, supervisors and managers, have great difficulty understanding each other and working together. Various psychological studies, including a recent one conducted at the General Services Administrations, offer an explanation for the problem. Because supervisors and managers see their own job futures differently, they react in opposite ways to various traditional job ideas such as "Promotions are based on ability and talents" or People who do a good job are rewarded."

Managers tend to believe these job concepts. Supervisors don't. As first-line supervisors see it, supervisors live in a kind of no-man's-land. Supervisors aren't bottom-rung employees and yet they're not allowed the planning or decision-making freedom or promotion potential that managers/executives have.

Because supervisors feel that their own promotion chances are so restricted and that their talents never will be fully evaluated, they regard pep talks in which managers imply "People who do a good job will be rewarded" or "Promotions are based on ability and talent" as unrealistic. As a result, say behavioral science experts Frank T. Paine and Martin J. Gannon, organization efficiency and performance suffer while supervisors concentrate, not on the managers' goals, but on their own definition of attainable success: "security, respect, and happiness." Since managers do have broad future opportunities, they tend to believe their own pep talks and mistakenly think their supervisors also believe them.

According to the psychologists, until management introduces new policies which allow supervisors to agree that "high performance will pay off for me," managers will continue to pep-talk about extra effort and improved efficiency but supervisors may not listen.

## How to Cope with the "It-Won't-Work" Employee

When a subordinate challenges a supervisor's plan on the grounds that "it won't work" or "we haven't the time," the supervisor's natural reaction is irritation.

The difference between the effective supervisor and the one who feels confused and thwarted is attitude and control. Robert W. Dorman, an executive development expert writing in *Advanced Management Journal*, warns that a supervisor "must pause and find words" to express his awareness of an opposing viewpoint—even if the subordinate's resistance is not logical. By pausing, the supervisor suggests thoughtfulness, concern, and constructive interest. "Well, I know you have given this some thought," he may say. Or, "There are certainly some difficulties and problems in this plan. . . ." The mood created by the pause and such words calms everyone's emotions. Reasoning is again possible and the supervisor can continue to explain his ideas.

## Tips on Sizing Up a Part-Time Worker

Suppose you have to choose between two applicants for the same part-time job. One is unmarried and attends school part-time. The other is married, has children, and does not attend school. Which one would probably stay with the job longer?

Psychologists have discovered that traditional ways of judging part-timers (by years of education, sex, marital status, children vs. no children, etc.) are all useless. None of these things has an effect on whether a part-timer quits quickly or stays for years. The researchers found only five guidelines that can be used. The part-timers who stay for long periods rate themselves on personality tests as having (A) good intelligence, (B) initiative, (C) self-assurance, and (D) a liking for their current part-time job which they consider "better than any other kind of work that I am qualified to do."

Age was the fifth guideline: The older the part-time worker, the more likely he/she will stay.

## Do Sales Contests Work?

Win a trip to Spain, a sports car, a boat, a color TV!

Contests for salespeople offer tempting prizes, but do they really make them work *harder?* There are three different kinds of people who sell: commission, salary-only, and salary-and-incentive. They have three different reactions to contests.

A consulting team of experts in business motivation and pay has analyzed the sales payment plans of eighty different industries, including durable and non-durable, finance, utility, and insurance. They found commission-only salespeople usually have a short training time, own their own autos, pay their own expenses, have no college degree, and have a very high earnings potential, up to $75,000 annually. They usually react favorably to some form of contest.

Salary-only salespeople often have completed some college and probably have a degree. Their annual salary is in the teens, they drive a company car, and are paid for expenses. They make customer calls on a weekly or monthly basis, and many sales take a week or more to complete. This kind of salesperson will not react favorably to sales contests, which they view as "gimmicks." The only kind of contest that might work with them is one involving short-term accomplishment with cash prizes.

Of all the people who sell, the salary-and-incentive workers are the most satisfied with their jobs. But their typical income is the lowest of the three groups. Though their daily routine is similar to their salary-only colleagues, their reaction to sales contests varies. High school graduates are very likely to find contests attractive. College graduates tend to avoid them.

Exactly why the three kinds of salespeople react so differently is not yet known.

## A Clumsy Dismissal Can Backfire

Maybe you never thought of it before, but you can make trouble for yourself when you fire someone—if you don't know how to do it properly. Ex-employees who have had their egos shattered by clumsy firing techniques sometimes make off with mailing lists, files, and technical data in order to get even.

Some experts suggest that when you tell people you are letting them go, you soften the blow by mentioning severance, bonus, vacation, and retirement money which they will receive. If they are cost-cutting victims, make that clear and save them the pain of thinking they've been incompetent. Your unpleasant task will be easier and more merciful if undertaken late in the afternoon and out of range of eavesdroppers. And even if the subordinate loses his temper and becomes abusive, keep calm. By losing your temper, you'll only be encouraging the get-even schemes you're trying to avoid.

## Making the Grapevine Work for You

Since the office grapevine is probably never going to be eliminated, learn how to turn it into an asset by making it work to your advantage.

Communication experts suggest that you think of the grapevine as your early warning system. Keep in mind that grapevine talk often has at least a kernel of truth, and some is surprisingly accurate. If nothing else, you can get a good idea of co-workers' personalities, fears, and ambitions by noticing the way each person talks up, ignores, alters, or reacts to various grapevine tales. Also, sifting through the rumors and gossip to find the kernel of truth can have other uses. It can keep you aware of what topics are being thought about and talked about by people in positions above and below you.

When something inaccurate about *you* comes along, denying it won't be enough. You must see that the true facts reach the people involved, especially your supervisors. If you're a supervisor and your people are being misled, you may have to reveal a decision earlier than you intended. For example, a slump in sales starts the rumor that there's going to be a layoff. In response, you may have to circulate the truth two weeks earlier than you planned: "We're eliminating all overtime at the end of the month until sales pick up. But no layoffs!"

By this prompt action, you've made the grapevine an asset. With the grapevine's warning, you've been able to improve output for the next two weeks by eliminating layoff worries, and you've put people's minds back where they belong—on their jobs!

## What Causes Those Resentments Between You and Your Boss?

People sometimes forget that "I hate my boss" can cut two ways. You can slam your hand on your kitchen table and announce to your sympathetic family, "I hate my boss." But if you have even one helper at your factory job, or one secretary or clerk at your office or sales position, or one assistant at your craft work, or a single volunteer committee member under your direction at your civic, religious, or cultural club, then *you're* a "boss" —just as surely as the person who sits in a carpeted office overseeing hundreds. It's a twinge of a different sort to contemplate how often the person you supervise may have said, "I hate my boss" about you!

Is hating your boss inevitable? Is it a normal reflex reaction to authority? "No. It's a sign of something wrong between two particular individuals, and there are many possible ways to prevent the conflict or ease it after it's once begun," says Dr. Joel Moses, who is Supervisor of Personnel Research for the mammoth AT&T corporation. Dr. Moses' specialty is identifying management potential by analyzing a person's interests, abilities, and motivations. In a special interview with Dr. Moses, surprising facts emerged about bosses and workers and about qualities that make a supervisor both likeable and successful.

If he/she just doesn't ruin it, says Dr. Moses, the boss has all the cards stacked in his/her favor. The people he/she is going to supervise will be anxious to be friends when they first meet their boss. They know their jobs depend on good relations with their supervisor. The very fact that a person has won the job of supervisor is impressive, and the title strengthens the initial favorable impression the boss makes. "If they have the job, they must know what they are doing" is the natural first reaction of those working for a supervisor. "Job charisma," Dr. Moses calls it.

But job charisma can fade. Bosses who give conflicting orders, who do not adequately explain what they want, or who do not recognize good work when they see it, shake their subordinates' confidence in their ability. The moment a subordinate comes to believe his boss is incompetent, an "I hate my boss" situation is born. Dishonesty in work relationships is equally corrosive. For example, said one executive we interviewed, if a work crew sees that the foreman regularly favors a certain man, the crew can't possibly respect or like that foreman.

In white-collar positions, bosses are looking for grief when they schedule weekend or late-hour dinner meetings for routine business. And they are seeking out trouble when they insist on parking space Number One while circulating a "parking spaces will no longer be assigned" memo for everyone else. In situations such as these, where they flaunt their power, they are exasperating those under them into an "I hate my boss" attitude. Similarly, it may be office politics or a yen to command that causes some supervisors to everlastingly modify and one-up their subordinates' decisions. Whatever the origin, such behavior guarantees frustration and anti-boss rumblings.

If you're a brand-new supervisor, psychologists have found that you can forestall anti-boss sentiment when you take over. Saying little and simply following established routine until you know your people as individuals help to encourage acceptance for yourself. If your predecessor was a success, then you are probably starting with workers who know what is required of them. If your predecessor was a crank or a failure, then you're bound to appear to all as a potential improvement. Unless you have been hired to cope with a crisis situation, insisting on sweeping method changes when you first arrive is a mistake. It will only ignite wildfire hostility as everyone begins to fear a shake-up in his own job.

And where there's hostility, there's action. If you dislike your own boss, you may not realize it, but you are expressing your feelings in one or more subtle ways during your workday. When a supervisor is bedeviled by excessive subordinate complaints, absenteeism, pilfering, and work slovenliness, he is being told off indirectly by people he has alienated. Someone who becomes thoroughly unhappy about his supervisor usually takes unsubtle, open action. He finds himself another position and quits.

Like Dagwood Bumstead, the unhappy subordinate may daydream about getting a new job and storming in to tell off the boss. Yet he'll probably never do it. Instead of a nose-to-nose shouting finale, industrial studies reveal that the job-quitting explanation will be mild: "This is too far to commute" or "I didn't like the work too much." This is not because the average person is afraid; it is because he is practical. As he sees it, "I'm getting out of here anyway. Maybe the boss'll be good for a reference some day. What have I got to gain from a commotion?"

One of the best ways to promote your own contentment with

your job is to try to understand your bosses and the pressures they face. One man, Gerald Suste, a forty-five-year-old executive vice-president, began as a fifteen-year-old errand boy earning money for college. As Mr. Suste moved up from manual work to supervisory positions, he observed the supervisor-subordinate relationship from many angles. You have to remember, says he, that if the boss is putting pressure on you to produce, it's because he has his own problems of deadlines, profits, and budgets. He probably even has *his* own boss.

Though hating the boss is not the normal reflex reaction of the vast majority of people, there is an unfortunate minority of people who have never learned to live with authority. As youngsters they never adapted to the requirements of parents or teachers; as adults they struggle with difficult work-adjustment problems. For this minority, the boss steps into the role of the parent with whom they have always battled. Seething with years of un-resolved anger, they are quick to take offense. "Who does the boss think he is? He can't tell me to do that! I quit!" Every personnel department is familiar with these workers. For them therapy is usually necessary.

How does the average person feel about his boss? Tomorrow morning, when you join the back-to-work rush hour, you can look around and be sure of the answer. Psychologists tell us that the average person has a tremendous ability to adjust to temporary frustration. However, they remind us that, in a mobile society such as ours, most people remain on a job only if that position offers more satisfactions than dissatisfactions. The truly unhappy subordinates leave. "My boss? Oh, she's/he's O.K." would be the reaction of the great majority of people you'll meet tomorrow. It's the attitude most workers instinctively long for, and, because of effort on both sides, it is achieved.

# Analyze Yourself: 8
## Match Your Job to Your Personality

Many people think matching your job to your personality is a "frill." This mistaken belief can keep them in the wrong job and bring them years of unnecessary unhappiness. The problem results from the popular belief that "people can do anything they put their minds to."

It's true men and women may perform passably in an uncongenial occupation. But when each day's work demands the suppression of basic temperament and talents, the toll in personal anguish is high. Intelligence has nothing to do with it. Personality, personal values, and inborn aptitudes do.

Tell a roomful of people, "I don't have the ability to become a professional musician or professional commercial artist," and no one will argue with you. No one will reply that it's "just a matter of putting your mind to it." No one will insist that you "just aren't trying." Most people accept the fact that musical ability and painting/drawing ability are inborn, that without the natural aptitude neither instruction nor willpower is sufficient.

But tell people that you cannot be a bookkeeper because you lack the finger dexterity to turn out a meticulous account page or because your high imagination causes your mind to wander when it is tied to routine work, and they'll become impatient. "It's just a matter of concentrating," they're likely to say.

Industrial psychologists have discovered that different kinds of work demand different inborn abilities and personality traits. No job is suitable for everyone. This section discusses many types of work, and the personal and inborn characteristics you need to succeed at and really enjoy the different occupations.

As you read, keep another fact in mind. For job satisfaction, not only must you match your job to your personality and talents, you must match it to your personal goals and values. Ultimately, you are the only person who can judge how "good" a job is. What your friends or family might describe as a very good position might seem like a so-so job to you.

Why the different reactions? Because *different people seek different work satisfactions, and many of these work-satisfaction goals are in conflict.*

For example, some people yearn for security above all else. Others consider security expendable; they want opportunity for promotion. Some thrive on predictable routine; they want each day to be like the day before. Others consider routine to be anathema; they long for constant challenge, for everything to be open-ended.

Other contrasting job goals: jobs with lots of people-contact vs. jobs where you are left alone in peace and quiet to do your work without constant interruptions; jobs where you really enjoy the daily activity vs. ones where it doesn't really matter what the work is as long as it's legal and high-paying.

You can only match your job to yourself if you first honestly analyze who you are and what you're after. This section will help you do that.

### Does Your Job Suit Your Personality?

You may have the ability to do a certain kind of work but not the personality for it.

Basically, you have to discover which of the two different kinds of job personalities you have. One kind of person needs people and enjoys working with others. People like this usually conform to others around them and don't take criticism and personality clashes to heart. This kind of person is happy in selling, executive positions, or any job that is done in a group.

The other kind of person often has the intelligence for executive work but is vaguely dissatisfied with it. People like this are upset by people-friction and are not conformists. They are happiest working at some kind of specialty where they can concentrate on their task, not on other people. The professions are good for them, as are the arts or research.

Many of us drift into work that is wrong for our personality because of some kind of pressure. A shy child might enter a by-yourself kind of work when he really needs a people-filled one. The individualist who is a school leader may be pushed into people-involved executive work when really his school leadership is the result of excelling at school projects—which suggests he might be happiest in a more private career. Finally, many people end up in the wrong job simply because of family pressure.

### Are You in the Wrong Job?

Many people make the mistake of choosing mechanical work just because they are good at working with their hands. But the Human Engineering Laboratories, which have tested over half a million people for job aptitudes, warn that this is a common error. Being good with your hands indicates only skillful fingers. Mechanical work is for you only if those skillful fingers are accompanied by a brain that is capable of visualizing a three-dimensional object. Often, say the laboratory experts, the two skills do *not* go together!

Similarly, others embark on a science career because they enjoy general science courses. Interest in these courses means only that one has a good reasoning ability which, again, may or may not be accompanied by the ability to visualize structures that is vital to a successful scientist.

And don't blame your son if his father is a mechanical whiz and he can't even understand a diagram. Being able to picture the structure of an object, which goes with understanding diagrams and blueprints, is a talent that a mother may pass on to a son, but which a boy can never inherit from his father. Those at the laboratory point out that the talent to mentally picture an object is a "sex-linked recessive trait passed from mother to son, never from father to son." However, girls are able to inherit this ability from either mother or father.

The Human Engineering Laboratories, also known as the Johnson O'Connor Research Foundation, are located at:

Suite 340
3445 Peachtree Rd., N.E.
Atlanta, Ga. 30326

Suite 124
2055 South Gessner
Houston, Tex. 77063

347 Beacon St.
Boston, Mass. 02116

1349 West Fifth St.
Los Angeles, Cal. 90017

161 East Erie St.
Chicago, Ill. 60611

11 East 62nd St.
New York, N.Y. 10021

47 East Adams St.
Detroit, Mich. 48226

3004 Sixth Ave.
San Diego, Cal. 92103

650 South Henderson St.
Fort Worth, Tex. 76104

906 South Cheyenne St.
Tulsa, Okla. 74119

121 Second St., N.E.
Washington, D.C. 20002

## What It Takes to Succeed as a Secretary or an Office Worker

Many people become secretaries. Some are happy and successful in their work; others, who are just as intelligent, are restless and dissatisfied. Why? The Johnson O'Connor Human Engineering Laboratories, a non-profit group which has tested half a million people for job aptitudes since 1922, has an explanation: It's a matter of your natural abilities and your basic personality. A good secretary, they told us, needs clerical ability, a natural ease in dealing with paperwork, figures, and symbols, as well as high finger dexterity. Without the clerical ability, she/he makes mistakes, falls behind, daydreams, and is just plain unhappy. Without finger dexterity, a secretary never masters the skills well enough to enjoy the work. In her book, *Be Yourself*, which reports on Johnson O'Connor career research, Margaret Broadley explains that clerical workers and private secretaries need two different kinds of basic personalities. To spend hours typing, doing accounts, running machines, or performing other solitary tasks, clerical workers need a "subjective" personality which makes them enjoy concentrating on the task at hand rather than working with people. A private secretary needs to enjoy dealing with people. If she has independent responsibilities for various activities, a secretary also needs a good amount of inductive reasoning talent—i.e., the ability to form a logical conclusion from scattered facts. Certain other qualities will interfere with a secretary's concentration, and will make her restless and bored. High creativity or a strong talent for thinking in three dimensions, or high ability to think ahead and foresee situations coupled with a strong inner drive to succeed, all make a secretary constantly restless for new challenges and finally make her dissatisfied with the career she's chosen.

In addition to secretarial work, there are, of course, millions of other office clerical positions. Unfortunately, many men and women who disliked reports and paperwork in high school or college turn to office employment when they leave the classroom. Then, if they are dissatisfied with their jobs or their performance in those jobs, they may worry about their capabilities in general.

To succeed at any kind of office paperwork, you need the

same high finger dexterity and strong natural talent for dealing with symbols and figures and paperwork that secretaries must have. If school reports and the like irritated you, office jobs are probably not your best career possibility.

## Clues to Your Hidden Job Abilities

"I don't like my job. But I don't know what kind of work I'd like any better" is a common complaint.

Paying attention to the things that give you trouble on the job and things that you succeed at off the job can help you discover your hidden job abilities and needs. For example, you may often fall behind at work because you're tempted to spend time away from your work station or desk on various errands and discussions. Ask yourself if all that talk and errand-hopping is really necessary. Or is it just a way to provide yourself with the human contact you enjoy? If you eventually realize that you're most content when dealing with people, and restless when confined for a long time to tools, papers, and objects, you've learned something valuable about yourself. You're now ready to improve your daily job life by seeking a job working with people which will satisfy your hidden work needs—a job in sales, for example.

Your activities at your church, lodge, union, political organization, or town youth group can provide other useful clues to the kind of job you would enjoy. If you're pleased when you're elected treasurer or financial leader of the group and enjoy the hours you spend performing your duties, realize that most people would shy away from such volunteer tasks. Your liking for the job probably reflects bookkeeping, numerical, or business talent. Do you find it easy to take on the role of chairperson and keep your committee working enthusiastically? You may have two precious talents on which you could build your paid work life: ability to work with people and organizational skill. Does arranging for publicity for your group or preparing its newsletter seem a fun and easy assignment? You probably would be happy working in some aspect of communications or public relations.

Overall, the responsibilities you accept as a pleasure and succeed at in your volunteer leisure activities suggest your hidden job abilities.

### Are You Trapped in a Non-Imaginative Job?

Were you always scolded for forgetfulness when you were a child? "If your head wasn't attached to your shoulders, you'd forget it." Now, at work, you probably find that your mind continues to wander. You lose track of where you were or, worse yet, make mistakes.

The Johnson O'Connor Human Engineering Laboratories have discovered that what is condemned as absentmindedness is often a powerful imagination and a rich flow of ideas trapped in the wrong job. Jobs that demand a steady level of straightforward concentration and in which a strong imagination can be a handicap include accountant, bookkeeper, key-punch operator, computer programmer, business executive, banker, typist, auditor, lawyer, administrator, physician, manager, and supervisor. High-imagination people do well in teaching, selling, writing, designing, interviewing, or any occupation that gives them an opportunity to talk with people and to think up new ideas, techniques, products, or methods.

If you're an imaginative person who has spent years obtaining training and experience in a non-imaginative occupation and you are now dissatisfied, you can salvage your training. An accountant could turn to teaching accounting; an administrator, executive, or supervisor could seek a position in an innovative industry or in marketing.

## What Kinds of Men Make Very Successful Salesmen?

In a survey that considered only men, a University of Chicago group of researchers came up with some unexpected facts about successful salesmen. Even if you've spent years working with salesmen, you may find the following very surprising.

There are, it turns out, some definite personality differences between the salesman who is moderately successful and the one who is very successful. But the differences are probably not what you'd expect. First of all, there's no great difference in the amount of "drive" the two types of people have. Nor does the fact that one has a college degree mean very much for sales success. It is also rather unimportant that one may have participated in extracurricular or athletic activities while in school.

At the Industrial Relations Center of the University of Chicago, the researchers believe they have found three characteristics that are typical of those salesmen who are more successful than the average. The most important trait seems to be a very strong sense of personal financial responsibility. This means they manage their own personal income well. They earn, invest, save, and accumulate. Next, these very successful salesmen married early and began their families early. The quick arrival of their babies meant that at an early age the fathers were usually their family's sole provider. Now, as successful salesmen, their greatest interest outside of work is family activities.

The better salesman's third predictable characteristic is stability. He has achieved stability in his work because of his past history of good performance. His current concern is to keep what he has gained rather than to plan for improvement or development.

Probably not the kind of personality most people would expect of the "successful" salesperson, is it?

### Foreman: Tougher Job than Company President?

In some ways it may be easier to be president of a company than a foreman of a work group. Industrial psychologists often rate being a foreman as the most difficult of all supervisory positions. Most supervisory positions allow time for a good amount of quiet paperwork. But the foreman's main activity all day long is face-to-face confrontations. Without great skill in human relations, a foreman cannot succeed.

People who were leaders in high school activities, it has been found, often make excellent foremen. They may not have earned the best school marks, but their ability to start and keep people moving on various school projects indicates they have an instinct for human relations and a talent for directing others.

"The Foreman's Letter" is a twice-monthly, four-page publication which specializes in job ideas to help foremen handle people and succeed in their work. "The Foreman's Letter" is available to any supervisor or member of a company who requests it (use company stationery). Address:

"The Foreman's Letter"
24 Rope Ferry Rd.
Waterford, Conn. 06386

## How to Find Low-Supervision, High-Freedom Jobs

Many people hate their jobs because they can't stand being closely supervised. They dislike being confined to one spot in one building and feel frustrated because they never see the finished product of their labor. Though they're miserable with their job conditions, they can't imagine any escape. "I haven't got a college education. So what else is there that gives you freedom of movement except selling? And I'm not the salesperson type," they say.

Yet there is a whole range of well-paying occupations which permits great freedom of movement and which provides the pleasure of doing a job from beginning to end with nobody checking on you every minute. If you're skillful with your hands and you enjoy working with things, consider becoming any of the following: an air-conditioning, refrigeration, or heating mechanic; an appliance, business machine, or electric-sign serviceperson; a millwright; a television and radio service technician; a truck or bus mechanic; an industrial machinery repairperson; a vending machine mechanic.

Though most of these jobs are commonly thought of as men's work, the Department of Labor suggests that the majority of repair occupations require relatively little physical strength. And research has shown that the same high finger dexterity which allows women to excel at factory assembly jobs also enables them to do very well at these high-paying repair occupations.

## Are You Unhappy at Work Because You "Don't Belong"?

You may be satisfied with your paycheck and with your job, yet find each morning that the thought of going to work depresses you. Why? The problem may be how you feel about your co-workers and how they feel about you.

Industrial psychologists have proved that to be happy on a job you must know that you "belong," that you are accepted by your co-workers. Psychologists have also discovered that all of us have a strong desire to be proud of the people we work with. Perhaps you do not have this feeling of pride. Perhaps the personalities and/or behavior standards of those you work with are seriously different from your own.

No matter how you try to hide your feelings about others, they will surely sense your true reaction to them. And this will create a barrier, turning you into an "outsider." It's a basic fact of human nature that, in order to have yourself accepted into a group, you in turn have to accept the group. One typical example: On a new job you may discover that the standard employee attitude toward the company is negative. You either go along with the gripes and adopt the group's negative viewpoint or you quickly find yourself living the "outsider" life.

If you believe you never will see the job as your present co-workers do or if you're genuinely uncomfortable with them because of other of their ideas and attitudes, consider finding work elsewhere. Elsewhere the workers may hold views compatible with your own and then you can mutually relax and accept each other.

### Rate Yourself: Can You Cope with Business Risks?

You may dream of someday starting your own business or leaving your routine job for a higher-risk, higher-potential job. But do you have the personality and temperament that can live comfortably with the paycheck insecurity that often accompanies such businesses?

Psychological experiments at the University of California indicate that people who cannot adjust to job insecurity have temperaments which they themselves describe as cooperative, determined, deliberative, efficient, self-controlled, poised, and stable. People who can take business risks in their stride tend to see themselves as being important, courageous, sharp-witted, clear-thinking, imaginative, ingenious, and foresighted. Which type of person are you?

To help you further evaluate your chances of success, the U.S. Small Business Administration (SBA) has a self-rating questionnaire dealing with *entrepreneur characteristics* you need to make a business succeed. The SBA says that among other things you must be a self-starter who likes people, decision-making, and responsibility. To test your attitude toward responsibility they ask you to choose one of the following statements:

1. "I like to take charge of things and see them through."
2. "I'll take over if I have to, but I'd rather let someone else be responsible."
3. "There's always some eager beaver around wanting to show how smart he is; I say, let him."

Did you answer No. 1? Then you have the entrepreneur attitude. But if you chose No. 3, better keep working for someone else! *Home Office Report,* a newsletter for self-employed business people has developed its own definition of the very special kind of person who is well suited to self-employment: He or she is the farsighted, free-thinking individual who wants to make it big without having to follow the usual, slower up-through-the-ranks routes. You can obtain the detailed SBA self-rating "Checklist for Going into Business," Small Marketers Aid No. 71, free by writing:

> SBA
> 1441 L St., N.W.
> Washington, D.C. 20416

### Business Men vs. Business Women: Any Differences?

Except for one thing, women business owners "are not much different" from men who set up their own businesses, according to a Center for Venture Management study.

But both men and women entrepreneurs are different from the average jobholder. If you stop to notice, you'll find that the business owners you know, both men and women, overwhelmingly come from a family where a parent had an independent business or an independent professional career. "What is happening is that entrepreneurs beget entrepreneurs," say the investigators. Unlike most jobholders, they're moderate to high risk-takers—that is, they see the risk, but it doesn't worry them. Hard drivers who love to work, they all have a tendency to marry themselves to their business at the expense of their flesh-and-blood husbands and wives. You may hear them talking about retiring, but so total is their dedication that they rarely do so. Even if they sell their business, you'll find they almost always start another one. As employees before they began their own businesses, they were restless, with a tendency to have a number of different jobs. Pleasant people to be around, and optimistic and positive about the present and future, you'll seldom find them dwelling on the past.

The one difference between the men and women? The women business owners enjoyed and profited from their years of schooling, while the men frequently chafed under it. The male entrepreneurs you know often have a school expulsion or drop-out episode buried under their well-earned business success.

### Would You Be Happy on a Space Mission?

Ever think of getting away from it all someday as a member of a crew on an orbiting space laboratory, a lunar colony, or an undersea station? Once aboard, do you think you'd be happy cooped up with the same companions and with a tight daily routine?

To find out how different kinds of personalities react to confined living conditions, scientists did research with people posted to small, isolated Antarctic stations. Working under a U.S. Navy fund grant, the scientists investigated conditions over a six-year period.

Measure yourself against the Antarctic personnel who were happy and successful in their isolated environment: Are you calm and even-tempered? Could you honestly say you are friendly, popular, likeable, and considerate of others? Are you also industrious, hardworking, motivated, proficient, and able to accept authority well? If you're weak in any of these traits, find another way to escape from it all and leave long-term space missions, undersea stations, etc., to those rare people who have all the required social, emotional, and work skills.

## Why Young People Keep Quitting Jobs

You meet your friend at the neighborhood shopping center and remember that his son started a new job recently. "How does Bill like the trucking company?" you ask. Your friend shrugs. "He quit. Now he's decided to study for a real estate license." You wonder what to say. During the last three years you know that Bill, who is now twenty-three, has started and quit five different kinds of jobs and careers. "We just can't get him to stick to anything," your friend tells you. "My wife is awfully upset!"

It may console Bill's parents and the parents of the hordes of other twenty to twenty-four-year-olds who keep changing their career plans to know that Bill's behavior is not unusual. Nor is his job-hopping likely to continue indefinitely! U.S. labor statistics reveal that men and women in this age bracket do more job-switching and career-changing than any other group. At that age, most are still without heavy family responsibilites and are still free to "try on" different careers for fit. This "trying on" of different occupations can seem strange or even wrong to older people, who were often forced by economic conditions to stay put in whatever career or job they first tried. Under today's more mobile conditions, most young people eventually find a job or career niche that suits them.

So, instead of despairing, friends and families can regard the twenty to twenty-four-year-olds' job-switching search as a healthy sign that often ends in success.

### Does Early Retirement Work?

Under certain conditions, most people who've tried early retirement do seem to like it. In a major investigation conducted over a period of years by the University of Michigan's Institute for Social Research, there were careful, personal interviews of automobile workers who retired between the ages of fifty-eight and sixty-five. Most people (89 percent) were glad they retired when they did, and said, "I'd recommend early retirement to others." The people interviewed made it clear that they don't become bored with retirement. A very popular sentiment was: "I liked it right away. And I like it even more now."

Poor health was the only condition that definitely lowered a person's satisfaction with retired life. The essentials for enjoying retirement were, first and foremost, having an adequate financial income; having retired as planned, rather than unexpectedly; and being active. A retired person's activity could be work around his/her own home, volunteer charity work, leisure amusements, socializing with others, or keeping up with the news. Private non-paid activities were just as satisfying to retired people as part-time work for money. The key to a satisfying early retirement seemed to be financial security, continued activity of some kind, and continued participation in life.

### How to Cure Yourself of "Job Blues"

If you have the "job blues," you are not alone. Job blues are quite common. People suffering from the blues describe it as feeling hopelessly trapped in a very boring, dead-end job. But after thoroughly investigating 1,095 workers and the blues, the Institute for Social Research at the University of Michigan had some cheerful findings. Contrary to the popular idea, your feelings of defeat about your work have very little to do with your age, sex, race, education, number of dependents, income, or collar color. People in dull white-collar jobs get the blues as well as high-income workers on tedious assembly lines.

"It's the characteristics of your particular job situation more than anything else that give you the blues. Education for a new kind of work is not always necessary—sometimes you can cure yourself by finding a new employer with a different attitude. Or, another solution would be finding a different kind of work which uses other skills and interests you already have. The things that the Institute found most important to combat the blues were jobs in which: your skills are fully used; you get enough help to do your work well; you have enough tools/machinery or equipment to work well; you receive relatively many types of fringe benefits; and you have a supervisor who leaves you alone unless you want help.

The more closely your new job resembles these conditions, the more quickly you will cure your job blues.

## Career Dreams That Backfire

Thinking big about your job future can be fun. It can even be useful if it encourages you to make practical plans for finding and holding the kind of job you can enjoy. Some people, however, suffer a chronic sense of disappointment with themselves because they've allowed their career dreams to hide their real accomplishments.

Children commonly picture themselves as being important and famous when they grow up. Without realizing it, some adults go on measuring their achievements against that juvenile fantasy. No matter how they progress in their careers, if their efforts aren't earth-shaking enough to be featured in all the newspapers, they're afflicted with perpetual dissatisfaction. Other people ignore career opportunities available to them while they imagine how great things could be if only they could just get off somewhere and start over.

Perhaps the most frustrated career daydreamer is the man or woman who was the "Golden Boy" or "Golden Girl" in high school or college. The triumphs and admiration of early years often set up expectations of supersuccess that adult life can rarely provide. Until people who are caught up in these dreams understand what they are doing to themselves, they'll be unable to appreciate their real achievements.

## Why Do You Work?

Do you think you work for money? Yes, but. . . .

Whether we are aware of it or not, most of us are interested in much more than money. What makes a grand-prize lottery winner tell the newspaper interviewer that he will continue working? Why are millionaires willing to labor at all kinds of private and public tasks?

Behavioral psychologists have discovered that, apart from the obvious financial rewards, work satisfies us by giving us opportunities for socializing, a sense of achievement, and a chance for recognition by other people. When we succeed at work, we are able to enjoy the delicious feeling of thinking we are worthwhile people. Anyone who really enjoys his/her work has captured the top prize that work can offer. That person has found contentment through an occupation that provides a sense of self-fulfillment.

If you've ever wondered why you, yourself, stay at your present job even though you know you could earn more money elsewhere, this could be the explanation. Probably you've unconsciously realized that your present position, though moderate in the money it pays, is high in psychological income.

# Landing the Perfect Job for You 9

You'll enormously improve your chances of landing the job you want if you will reverse the usual job-hunting attitude. Instead of thinking about "why I want this job," concentrate on "what is it that they need that I can contribute?"

In order to answer the question accurately, you must put some effort into learning about the potential employer who has that "perfect" job for you. Because so few people are willing to prepare properly for an interview, you will stand out amidst the applicant mob if you take care of the preliminaries.

To prepare, you find out as much as you can about the responsibilities of the job; the department you would be in; who, specifically, makes the final job-hiring decision; the company's products; management goals; management philosophy; company size; its economic condition; executives; current problems; setbacks; triumphs. You come into possession of these answers by searching around among your acquaintances till you locate a few people who now work for or who have worked for the company. If necessary, you keep searching until you find someone who knows someone who knows someone who knows someone who works there. Then you meet with these people, in person if possible, on the phone if necessary. You explain you're interested in a job with that organization and you want to be intelligent about the organization during your interview. Most people sympathize when you mention an interview and are glad to discuss your questions.

Always seek out at least two people—in fact, the more people the better. Each will answer the questions somewhat differently and you'll develop a more rounded, truer picture. But never settle for just one background talk. One person's view of the organization may be distorted because of personal job problems and you'll come away totally misinformed. After your conversations, if you have important unanswered questions, you can supplement what you learned by inquiring at the local Chamber of Commerce and gleaning additional information from industrial directories and newspaper data available at the library.

All of this effort is worthwhile because when you sit down at the interview, you are then able to "speak their language." You are able to answer questions and present yourself in a way that matches their problems and needs.

Balance the two contrasting interviews in your mind for a minute—(A) Average interview: all about you, and (B) Prepared interview: all about the company and what you, the interviewee, can contribute to it. Obviously, which kind of interviewee is going to seem like "the right person for the job"?

So far we have discussed the essential basic attitudes you must bring with you to land that perfect job for you. The rest of this section offers you additional valuable techniques and facts which you can use to tip the final job-offer decision in your favor.

### Landing a Higher-Paying Job

When they seek a better job, most people depend solely on employment agencies and help-wanted ads. Yet the right kind of personal letter sent to selected company officials—who have *not* advertised any job—can be your best tool for obtaining a new position at a significant salary increase.

In his book, *The Professional Job Changing System*, Robert J. Jameson reports about his consulting experience with hundreds of job-changing campaigns involving salaries from $8,000 to

$50,000. "If you can generate an interview and impress an important executive with your ability, he'll find a way to take you aboard even if he has to create a job," says Mr. Jameson.

The most effective first letters, Jameson reveals, should not mention current or expected salary. Instead, in two pages of single-space copy, present your previous accomplishments, together with an explanation of what you think your skills and talents will contribute to the company to which you're applying. Address letters to specific executives by name, not simply by title. Obtain the names from *Standard & Poor's* or *Dun & Bradstreet's* directories of corporations, which are available at the public library.

Mr. Jameson has also discovered that letters written on 7 × 10 monarch-size stationery appear more personal and normally draw more response than 8 × 11-size letters. Light-colored paper may slightly outpull white. But bold, dark, or other strong colors always produce a lower response. If you're hunting in the $8,000–$20,000 range, a 6–8 percent response indicating some kind of interest is good; in the $20,000–$30,000, a 3–4 percent positive response to your letters is good. And, for some reason, signing your letter with a blue felt-tip pen seems to produce a signature that appeals to potential employers.

Once you learn to look for them there, you'll find job leads in your newspapers' business pages which feature news articles about newly promoted executives. These news features will mention nothing about other job offerings. But it is a fact of business life that newly promoted people commonly seek personnel from outside their company, so write to them. Letters to successful people who graduated from your school, especially if mailed to their home addresses, are also very productive.

If you think your age is a job-hunting problem—either too young or too old for the salary and position you seek—direct your campaign toward executives in your own age bracket or older. Your library's *Dun & Bradstreet Reference Book of Corporate Management* provides the birth dates of company officials.

If you don't hear from a firm in which you have a particular interest, follow up after three weeks with another letter restating your interest in the company and the contribution you could make. This frequently brings good results.

## Can You Fool the Personality Tester?

Nowadays when you apply for a job, you may have to take a personality test to see if you are suited to the position. Though critics complain that some of our greatest men—such as Lincoln, Edison, and Ben Franklin—would have flunked these conformist tests, many employers rely heavily on them. A recent experiment indicates that you can fool the test and load the answers in your favor only if you are sure of what characteristics the tester is seeking. For example, in a test for a sales position, the type of person being sought is an optimistic, outgoing, non-worrying, non-moody, and not easily discouraged extrovert. Salespeople are also supposed to be dominant and high on self-confidence.

Martin Gross, who made a three-year study of tests and how they're scored, reports in his book, *The Brain Watchers* (Random House), that to succeed with these tests you must present yourself as near perfect as possible in the traits the job requires. If you're seeking an executive position, you can be sure they're very interested in your desire for "achievement." If you work more for the pay and what it will buy rather than for achievement alone, don't admit it. The test may put some tough achievement choices to you, such as (A) I like to help my friends when they are in trouble, or (B) I like to do my very best in whatever I undertake. Choose the "achiever" answer—B.

If you're applying for a position where you think they're checking on the degree of your "masculinity," Mr. Gross suggests you choose the "virile" choices, no matter how childish they may seem. If you are asked the following, as on one test—Which do you like? (A) climbing along the edge of a precipice, (B) a bridge, (C) snakes, (D) detective stories, (E) social-problem movies, (F) art galleries, (G) pursuing bandits in a sheriff's posse, or (H) poetry —the "masculine" choices you should make are A, C, D, and G.

**Do People Tell the Truth
on Job Applications?**

Sorry, but the answer seems to be "only sometimes." So if you're doing the hiring, you may find it's best to check out key application answers. And if you're applying, you may want to stick closer to the facts from now on, because experienced employers are learning they do have to check.

The questions concerning previous salary and the length of time you were on your last job seem to be items you have to watch most closely. In one recent experiment, half of 111 job applicants stretched the length of their last employment by about sixteen months and almost three-fourths exaggerated their previous salary.

The answer to "Why did you leave your last position?" is obviously something a job applicant and his past employer may disagree about. And they do! You'll often find contrasting stories, such as that of the lady who claimed she had left because of "low salary," while her past employer said, "I fired her for breaking company rules." About one person in four had a different why-I-left story from the one offered by his or her former employer.

You can usually accept answers about positions held as being close to the truth. People probably figure that in this area there's no sense in wandering too far from the facts. Suppose, for example, you untruthfully said you'd been a welder and got the new job. What would you do when they expected you to start welding?

But employers should beware of becoming too cynical and sniffing suspiciously at all applicants and their completed job-application forms. The answers of approximately one out of every three people checked in the experiment turned out to be 100 percent accurate.

## Impressing the Job Interviewer

Whether you're being interviewed for a clerical, sales, factory, or executive job, you'll make your best impression if you remember that the interviewer is interested in what you can do for him/her. Many people lessen their chances by wasting valuable interview time talking about why they want the job. Interviewers aren't really interested in your personal dreams. You'll impress them best if you concentrate your discussion on how your experience, your training, and your attitude toward the job will be useful to the company.

Western Temporary, a nationwide placement service with 142 offices, has interviewed hundreds of thousands of job seekers. They suggest that many applicants fail to obtain the jobs they seek because:

1. They don't evaluate what they really can do and so unnecessarily belittle and underrate themselves.
2. They're not flexible enough. Job seekers often arrive at the meeting with a set idea of the kind of job they want. Though other excellent opportunities may be suggested by the interviewer, they won't readjust their ideas.
3. They give the impression they're "prima donnas." A "let's try it and see" attitude would take them a lot further.

Western also has discovered that you strengthen your chances of getting a job by leaving a complete written résumé with the interviewer and by being an interview early bird. Monday is better than Friday for interviews and morning ones go better than those that take place in the afternoon.

## The Vital First Five Minutes of a Job Interview

Up to now, you may have thought that the first few minutes of a job interview were the easiest. You and the interviewer are introducing yourselves and talking about general topics before settling down to serious details. Be careful, though. Those minutes are not only important, they are probably *it*. Industrial psychologists have found that most interviewers form a complete impression of you and your fitness for the job during the first four or five minutes of the interview. Regardless of what happens later, their initial reaction to you changes very little. It's not that the interviewer is being deliberately unfair. It's apparently just the way human nature works.

One possible guide to what impresses an interviewer during those opening moments comes from a study of people interviewing others for seven kinds of popular jobs: general manual work, clerk-typist, general management, management trainee, general sales, engineer, and secretary. The interviewers for all these jobs said they were impressed by evidence of a job applicant being stable, responsible, conscientious, and dependable. However, psychologists who studied the interviewers point out that it's not always easy for the interviewers themselves to be sure of what really does impress them during those first crucial four or five minutes.

## Getting the Job You Want

Though your job qualifications may be carefully considered, most employers' final decisions about whether to offer you the position are emotional, says career counsellor Eli Djeddah.

Said Mr. Djeddah during our interview, you must first know exactly what kind of job you are looking for. And you must have an effective written summary (or résumé) of your training and experience. Then you can strengthen the emotional impression you create by being careful of your personal appearance and *learning to listen.* "Remember that we were born with one mouth and two ears and not the opposite," says Mr. Djeddah.

As you listen to your prospective employers, they will automatically discuss the parts of the job which seem most important to them. You will then know which sections of your background to emphasize to match the job needs. Writing a thank-you note after an interview is often overlooked. Yet Eli Djeddah believes that for white-collar positions, the deciding factor in who gets the job has very often been the thank-you note. It's all part of the basic job-hunting fact: most final employment decisions about you are emotional.

## How the Temperature Can Affect Your Career

Your chances of winning the job you want or of favorably impressing a new client are best when the temperature-humidity index is comfortable. Psychological experiments at Kansas State University proved that temperature discomfort causes a definite drop in favorable decisions about other people. In other words, when the temperature is uncomfortable, people are likely to react negatively to you or to your proposal.

The researchers suggest that when you are going to be evaluated by someone, you should, if possible, provide comfortable temperature conditions. Meeting in an air-conditioned room or one with sufficient wintertime warmth makes it more likely that the other person will make a favorable decision about you.

## Want a Job? Why Not Offer a Reward?

The problem we all face is how to get to know the "right" people. As everyone realizes, many of the best jobs are never advertised. Soon after the openings develop, people who know about the vacancies tell friends, and the positions are quickly filled.

A brand-new way to tune yourself into this private someone-told-me-about-it job grapevine has been invented in southern Illinois. The method is simple and could work for anyone, anywhere. In addition, it costs far less than paying an agency fee; less, too, than plodding around for weeks searching for the better job you want. Here's how it works.

An ad was placed in the local newspaper offering a money reward to anyone who knew about good secretarial, truck driver, welder, bookkeeper, sales, factory, keypunch, nurse's aid, etc., jobs. The ad stated that the reward would be paid only if the information about the job opportunity led to someone's being hired. Information about job openings poured in. The ad *with* the reward feature produced in only one week ten times as many leads to good job openings as the same ad *without* a reward feature had produced in two weeks.

You don't have to depend on an agency placing a reward ad for you. You can write and place the ad yourself. Remember you're only going to have to pay that reward if you're hired for a new job. State that in your ad. Then offer whatever would be an appropriate reward in your area, and tune yourself into the good jobs that are being talked about in your town and surrounding area.

## Don't Train for the Wrong Job: Where the Jobs Will Be Between Now and 1985

If you're one of the millions of Americans aged seventeen to seventy who is either beginning to train for a particular career or is hoping to take new training and change the kind of work you do, be careful you don't fit yourself for a job where employment opportunities are decreasing! An 845-page government report, *Occupational Outlook Handbook 1974–1985*, discusses what job opportunities will be like between now and 1985. Following is the outlook for some of the popular occupations:

*Teachers:* Qualified candidates will exceed jobs. Badly overcrowded. Least competition for teachers of mathematics, industrial arts, special education, and some vocational-technical subjects.

*Truck Drivers:* For both local and long-distance truck drivers opportunities will be "moderate."

*Machine Tool Operators, Carpenters, Foremen:* Moderate opportunities. Greatest demand for carpenters will be in maintenance departments rather than in construction.

*Assemblers:* "Slow" growth; available jobs will come mainly from death and retirement of present workers.

*Lawyers:* The best prospects are for a new practice in suburbs or small towns. There is heavy competition for salaried city work.

*Electricians, Engineering and Science Technicians, Mechanics, and Repairpeople for air-conditioning, heating, computer service, industrial machinery;* and *Cosmetologists, Dental Assistants, Typists, Architects, Accountants (with college degrees), Dentists, Physicians, Systems Analysts, Social Workers (with graduate degrees):* All of these are and will be favorable growing fields with many job opportunities.

Some occupations will be both good and bad. You must pick the right specialty or have the required school degrees. For example:

*Medical Record Technicians:* May need a two-year college "associate" degree.

*Engineers:* Outlook is generally favorable, especially for new graduates with knowledge of recent techniques who can apply engineering principles to medical, biological, and other sciences.

*Secretaries, Shorthand Reporters:* Excellent prospects, but dictating machines will limit office-stenographer positions.

*Computer Operators:* Rapid rise for console and auxiliary-equipment operators, but declining need for keypunch personnel.

For facts about other occupations, consult the *Occupational Outlook Handbook 1974–1985*. Almost every library has it.

## How to Avoid the "Gyp" Trade Schools

If you are bored with your job or hungry for better-paying work, it may have occurred to you that a good-paying trade career might solve your problem. Your next step is finding a good trade school and avoiding the gyps.

In a unique and very helpful book, *If Not College, What? The Guide to Career Education*, Muriel Lederer has collected and clearly explained all you possibly need to know about two hundred trades and skills—how to learn them, what the work opportunities and salaries are, and what kind of personality you need to enjoy the work. During the years in which she researched the facts for her book, Ms. Lederer discovered how to recognize the telltale signs of the unreliable, "gyp" trade schools which take your money but do not fulfill their promises to you. Here are the precautions she recommends you take:

Watch out if the salespeople offer a "substantial" discount on tuition in exchange for immediate cash payment or if they insist that you make up your mind immediately because "there are only a few openings left" or because the salespeople are leaving the area for several months. Be suspicious of a school that makes extravagant claims for placement and employment, yet seems reluctant to give you names of graduates you can talk to for recommendations. If school officials discourage your attempt to visit the school beforehand, ask yourself why. Be on your guard if the school promises a fabulous career in a glamorous industry after only a few weeks' training or if a private correspondence course promises diplomas usually granted only by colleges and universities. Sure, you'll have the "diploma," but what employer will take it seriously? And when you see the words "registered," "approved," or "accredited" applied to a school, realize the words by themselves mean nothing. The school could be "registered, approved, and accredited" by the owner's mother and father! The question is: Approved, accredited, and registered by what agency or group?

Finally, does the school have a fair refund policy clearly stated in writing in its bulletin? Suppose you change your mind soon after the course begins. Without a clearly stated refund policy, you may find you are legally obligated to pay the entire tuition fee whether or not you take the course. Your local Better Business Bureau or Chamber of Commerce can tell you whether any complaints have been registered against the school; and for the real truth, ask employers in the field if they would hire someone who took that school's course.

Ms. Lederer's book is available in a hardcover and a softcover edition, both published by Quadrangle.

Two *free* directories of reliable schools are available upon request. (*Note:* There are other reliable schools which are not on these lists, but these directories will give you a good start.)

*Directory of Accredited Private Trade and Technical Schools*
(Rev. Ed.)
National Association of Trade and Technical Schools
2021 L St., N.W.
Washington, D.C. 20009

*Directory of Accredited Private Home Study Schools*
National Home Study Council
1601 18th St., N.W.
Washington, D.C. 20009

## Getting Ahead on the Job—No-Studying High School and College Credits

Is lack of a high school diploma or lack of college credits fencing you out of the job you want or the promotion you know you deserve? On the average, with one to three years of high school you'll earn $380,000 in your lifetime. With a high school diploma it rises to $478,000. Some college credits, one to three years, and your average earnings are $650,000. And a college diploma helps you to approximately $760,000.

You may be able to obtain a high school diploma or college credits, then move into the better job and earn the extra income without taking any courses and without going to classes. Those who feel they've learned through living and have neither the time nor patience for becoming students again may obtain a high school equivalency certificate by taking GED (General Education Development) tests. The high school equivalency certificate equals a diploma and is awarded by all state departments of education. Your local town board of education can give you information about where and when the exams are given. Usually you can obtain the facts quickly by telephone or you can write:

> GED Testing Service
> American Council on Education
> 1 DuPont Circle, N.W.
> Washington, D.C. 20036.

If it's college credit you want, there are the CLEP (College Level Examination Program) exams. Many men and women have absorbed through their jobs and through self-education the equivalent of freshman and sophomore college introductory courses. "Why should I have to sit through basic classes in business purchasing, the English novel, or Spanish, when I've been involved with it all these years and have already absorbed this material on my own?" they ask. CLEP examinations are for them. CLEP does not itself grant college credits, but more than thirteen hundred colleges and universities throughout the United States will give you credit toward a college degree based on your CLEP scores. Ask at your local community or four-year college, or write:

> CLEP
> Box 1821
> Princeton, N.J. 04540.

## Must You Really Be a Success by Age Forty?

You may have more time ahead of you than you think to pursue success.

Many people will tell you that if you haven't "made it" in your work by age forty, you're going to feel discouraged. But Dr. David Gutmann, a clinical psychologist who has been investigating the subject since 1956, reports that, psychologically, age forty is *not* the important age. Dr. Guttman has worked, not only with Americans, but with other groups around the world, and he finds that the age pattern everywhere is the same. It seems that up until about age fifty-five, men are aggressive and self-reliant in regard to their careers. After that, the average man usually stops seeing the world as something he can conquer and is often willing to adapt to conditions and act in a more careful way.

So far this age pattern for success is only true for men. The idea of careers for women is still so new that it has not yet been possible to discover women's age reaction to job success.

## How Your Job Can Lengthen Your Life

If you want to live to a ripe old age, make an effort to find a job you like and one that you can be proud of doing successfully.

A study of life expectancy conducted by a major life insurance company concluded that "it may well be that work satisfaction, together with public recognition of accomplishments, is an important determinant of health and longevity." Therefore, if you're known as one of the best mechanics in town or are recognized as a leader in your own specialty or business, you may be adding years to your life.

The insurance-company study uncovered other surprising facts: Contrary to the popular impression that top business executives are high health risks, these people actually have a death rate that averages one-third less through age eighty-five, when compared to American men in general. Investigations of "professional, technical and kindred workers" and of "managers, officials and proprietors" reveal that since they seem to be doing work they enjoy, they seem to thrive on their responsibilities. Though success and pride in other kinds of jobs have not yet been studied, presumably the same pattern would appear.

# NOTES AND SOURCES

## 1  Problem Co-Workers: How to Cope and Win

### Getting Along with the Know-It-All and the VIP

DR. EDWARD HODNETT, *The Art of Working With People* (New York: Harper & Brothers, 1959), pp. 50–52.

### People Who Can't Make Up Their Minds

GERALD D. BELL, *The Achievers* (Chapel Hill, N.C.: Preston-Hill, Inc., 1974).

### Drug Addicts Where You Work

"Drugs, Crime and Business," *Behavior Today*, vol. 3, no. 35 (August 28, 1972), p. 1. Report available from Levy, TFLI, 487 Park Ave., New York, N.Y. 10022.

"Clinical Bio-Tox Laboratories Survey," *Personnel Journal* (September 1972), p. 635.

### Alibi Joe: How Understanding Him Can Save You Grief

HARRY W. HEPNER AND FREDERICK B. PETTENGILL, *Perceptive Manage-*

*ment and Supervision—Social Responsibilities and Challenges.* 2d ed. (Englewood Cliffs, N.J.: Prentice-Hall, 1971), pp. 486–87.

### Why They're Not Telling You What They're Not Telling You

JOSEPH LEESE, "The Bureaucratic Colander," *Personnel Journal* (October 1974).

### Deciding About Your New Co-Workers

HENRY L. TOSI AND W. CLAY HAMMER, *Organizational Behavior and Management* (Chicago: St. Clair Press, 1974), pp. 194–95.

## 2 Promotion Strategies

### Business Clichés That Could Spell Trouble

FREDERICK E. FISHER, "Casting Out Organizational Demons: An Exorcise in Leadership," *Advanced Management Journal* (July 1974).

### Where Enemies Come From

ELTON T. REEVES, *So You Want to Be an Executive!* (New York: American Management Associations, Inc., 1971), pp. 94–96, 100–109.

### Should You Accept a Promotion?

"Closed Loop: Disenchantment," *MBA* (August/September 1973), p. 18.

### When Your Company Wants You to Relocate

The results of 11th Annual Survey of Corporate Moving Practices conducted during Winter of 1978 by Atlas Van Lines, Inc., Evansville, Indiana.

MARGARET E. BROADLEY, *Be Yourself: Analyzing Your Innate Aptitudes* (Washington, D.C.: Robert B. Luce, Inc., 1972).

*Note:* The book discussed above, *Be Yourself*, is the most useful and extraordinary book for the average person that I have found in the almost seven years of research I've done for *Jobmanship*. It's written in easy conversational layman's style throughout. I think many, many readers would find it enormously useful for understanding some of their own career problems and for helping their high school- and college-age children.

## 3 Making Things Break Your Way by Saying It Right

### · Why People Aren't Reasonable

DR. JESSE S. NIRENBERG, *Getting Through to People* (Englewood Cliffs, N.J.: Prentice-Hall, 1963), pp. 131–133.

### How to Deal With Hostile Questions

PAUL R. EDWARDS, "Nine Out of Ten Questions Don't Need an Answer," *Management Review* (November 1976), pp. 57–58, condensed from *Public Relations Journal* (July 1976).

### When There's Tension Between You and a Co-Worker

From a *Jobmanship* interview with Jesse S. Nirenberg, Ph.D., industrial psychologist and author of *Getting Through to People*.

### Avoiding Personality Hassles with People You Work With

From a *Jobmanship* interview with Dr. John L. Butler, industrial psychologist and principal of Ernst & Ernst, 150 South Wacker Drive, Chicago, Illinois, 60606.

### Keeping Personal Anger Out of Job Disagreements

WARREN H. SCHMIDT, "Conflict, a Powerful Process for (Good or Bad) Change," *Management Review* (December 1974).

### Asking for That Raise

"The Quest for the Sizable Paycheck," *Automation, The Production Engineering Magazine*, vol. 23, no. 4 (April 1976), pp. 52–56.

### When Your Boss Won't Give You a Raise

From a *Jobmanship* interview with Dr. Ernest Dichter, the internationally recognized "father of motivational research" and author of *Motivating Human Behavior* (New York: McGraw-Hill, 1971).

## 4 Shining Up Your Image

### "Meetingship": How to Make Yourself Look Good at a Meeting

MARTIN R. SMITH, *I Hate to See a Manager Cry* (Reading, Mass.: Addison-Wesley Publishing Co., 1973).

### Who Is Keeping You in the Background at Meetings?

RICHARD C. GROTE, "Why Meetings Jump the Track," *Supervisory Management* (January 1971).

### Which People Can You Trust?

DR. AINSLIE MEARES, *How to Be a Boss: A Practicing Psychiatrist on the Managing of Men* (New York: Coward, McCann, 1970).

### Hidden Causes: Why Are You Late for Work So Often?

"Outmaneuver the 10-Minute Latecomer," *Office Supervisor's Bulletin* (December 15, 1972), pp. 4–5.

### When You Play Hooky from Work

"Is an Employee Who Tells a Lie Entitled to 'Progressive Discipline'?" *Employee Relations in Action* (New York: Business Research Publications, Inc., July 1973).

### Don't Abuse Your Unemployment Benefits

South Dakota Commission Decision No. 2073-C-250.
"Can an Employee Force You to Fire Him So He Can Collect Unemployment Compensation?" *White Collar Management* (New York: Business Research Publications, Inc., March 1972).

## 5 Reading the Boss' Mind

### Deciphering the Boss' Hidden Messages

GERARD I. NIERENBERG AND HENRY CALERO, *Meta-Talk: Guide to Hidden Meanings in Conversations* (New York: Trident Press, 1973).

### Understanding Body Language

MERLYN CUNDIFF, *Kinesics* (West Nyack, N.Y.: Parker Publishing Company, Inc., 1972).

### Are You Having Trouble with Your New Boss?

HARRY LEVENSON, *Executive Stress* (New York: Harper & Row, 1964), p. 118.

### What Is Your Boss Afraid Of?

JOHN COWAN, "Fear and the Manager," *S.A.M. Adanced Management Journal* (July 1974), pp. 4–8.

## 6 Boss Troubles, and What to do About Them

### How Your Boss' Pay Affects Yours

PAUL S. GOODMAN, "Effect of Perceived Inequity on Salary Allocation Decisions," *Journal of Applied Psychology*, vol. 60, no. 3 (June 1975), pp. 372–375.

## 7 If You're a Supervisor

### The Ten Leading Gripes About Bosses

From a nationwide *Jobmanship* poll conducted in the more than 300 *Family Weekly* newspapers.

**Fourteen Complaints Secretaries Have About Bosses—and Some Solutions**

From a survey conducted for *Jobmanship* by Mrs. Irene Stone, editor of *P.S. for Private Secretaries* (Waterford, Conn.: Bureau of Business Practice, Inc.), through their "Secretarial Clinic" feature.

**On-the-Job Compliments: What's the Real Story?**

ARTHUR G. BEDEIAN, "Superior Subordinate Role Perception," *Personnel Administration and Public Personnel Review* (November/December 1972).

**How Supervisors Misunderstand What Workers Want**

URY M. GLUSKINOS AND BRUCE J. KESTELMAN, "Management and Labor Leaders' Perception of Worker Needs as Compared with Self-Reported Needs," *Personnel Psychology* (Summer 1971).

**Why Supervisors and Managers Don't Understand Each Other**

FRANK T. PAINE AND MARTIN J. GANNON, "Job Attitudes of Supervisors and Managers," *Personnel Psychology* (Winter 1973).

**How to Cope with the "It-Won't-Work" Employee**

ROBERT W. DORMAN, "Tighter, Tougher, Quicker, Smarter," *Advanced Management Journal* (October 1967).

**Tips on Sizing Up a Part-Time Worker**

MARTIN J. GANNON AND JOSEPH C. NORTHERN, "A Comparison of Short-Term and Long-Term Part-Time Employees," *Personnel Psychology* (Winter 1971).

**Do Sales Contests Work?**

JOHN W. ANNAS, "Profiles of Motivation," *Personnel Journal* (March 1973).

## 8 Analyze Yourself: Match Your Job to Your Personality

**Does Your Job Suit Your Personality?**

BROADLEY, op cit.

**Are You in the Wrong Job?**

Ibid.

**What It Takes to Succeed as a Secretary or an Office Worker**

Ibid.

**Are You Trapped in a Non-Imaginative Job?**

DEAN TREMBLY, *Concentration and Imagination* (Boston: Johnson O'Connor Research Foundation, Human Engineering Laboratory, Bulletin No. 112).

**What Kinds of People Make Very Successful Salesmen?**

MELANY E. BAEHR AND GLENN B. WILLIAMS, "Prediction of Sales Success from Factorially Determined Dimensions of Personal Background Data," *Journal of Applied Psychology* (1968 Volume), p. 98.

**How to Find Low-Supervision, High-Freedom Jobs**

"Summary of Job Prospects and Annual Openings for Selected Occupations Through Mid-1980's," Second in a three-part series, *Women & Work* (Washington, D.C., May 1974).

**Are You Unhappy at Work Because You "Don't Belong"?**

MARTIN M. BRUCE, PH.D., *Human Relations in Small Business*, Small Business Management Series no. 3 (Washington, D.C.: The Small Business Administration, 1969), p. 11.

### Rate Yourself: Can You Cope with Business Risks?

EDWIN E. GHISELLI, "Some Motivational Factors in the Success of Managers," *Personnel Psychology* (Winter 1968), p. 434.

LEON HENRY, JR., *Home Office Report* (17 Scarsdale Farm Rd., Scarsdale, N.Y. 10583).

### Business Men vs. Business Women: Any Differences?

JAMES W. SCHREIER, "Is the Female Entrepreneur Different?" *MBA* (March 1976), pp. 40–43.

### Would You Be Happy on a Space Mission?

E. K. ERIC GUNDERSON AND DAVID H. RYMAN, "Convergent and Discriminant Validities of Performance Evaluations in Extremely Isolated Groups," *Personnel Psychology* (Winter 1971).

### Why Young People Keep Quitting Jobs

CURTIS L. GILROY, "Job Losers, Leavers, and Entrants: Traits and Trends," *Monthly Labor Review*, vol. 96, no. 6 (August 1973), p. 5.

### Does Early Retirement Work?

RICHARD E. BARFIELD, *The Automobile Worker and Retirement: A Second Look* (Ann Arbor: Institute for Social Research, University of Michigan, 1970).

### How to Cure Yourself of "Job Blues"

STANLEY E. SEASHORE AND J. THAD BARROWE, "Demographic and Job Factors Associated with the 'Blue Collar Blues'," (Ann Arbor: Institute for Social Research, University of Michigan, March 1972).

## 9 Landing the Perfect Job for You

### Landing a Higher-Paying Job

ROBERT J. JAMESON, *The Professional Job Changing System* (Verona, N.J.: Performance Dynamics, Inc., 1976).

### Can You Fool the Personality Tester?

MARTIN L. GROSS, *The Brain Watchers* (New York: Random House, 1962).

WARREN S. BLUMENFELD, "Effects of Various Instructions on Personality Inventory Scores," *Personnel Administration* (September/October 1972).

### Do People Tell the Truth on Job Applications?

IRWIN L. GOLDSTEIN, "The Application Blank: How Honest Are the Responses?" *Journal of Applied Psychology* (October 1971).

### Impressing the Job Interviewer

"Everything You Always Wanted to Know About 'The Interview' But Were Afraid to Ask." Booklet issued by Western Temporary Services, Inc.

### The Vital First Five Minutes of a Job Interview

MILTON D. HAKEL AND ALLEN J. SCHUH, "Job Applicant Attributes Judged Important Across Seven Diverse Occupations," *Personnel Psychology* (Spring 1971).

E. C. WEBSTER, "Decision-Making in the Employment Interview" (Montreal, Canada: Industrial Relations Centre, McGill University, 1964).

### Getting the Job You Want

From a *Jobsmanship* interview with Mr. Eli Djeddah, president of Bernard Haldane Associates, San Francisco, and author of *Moving Up*.

### How the Temperature Can Affect Your Career

WILLIAM GRIFFIT, "Environmental Effects on Interpersonal Affective Behavior: Ambient Effective Temperature and Attraction," *Journal of Personality and Social Psychology*, vol. 15 (July 1970).

### Want a Job? Why Not Offer a Reward?

"Jobs for Sale," *Behavior Today*, vol. IV, no. 5 (January 29, 1973), p. 2.

### Must You Really Be a Success by Age Forty?

"Giving Up the Rat Race," *Behavior Today* (February 1972), p. 2.

### How Your Job Can Lengthen Your Life

"Longevity of Corporate Executives," *Statistical Bulletin*, published by Metropolitan Life Insurance Company, vol. 55, (February 1974), pp. 2–4.